CENTERING THROUGH WRITING

Right Brain/Left Brain Techniques Applied to Writing

Margaret Hatcher, Ed.D.

UNIVERSITY
PRESS OF
AMERICA

LANHAM • NEW YORK • LONDON

Copyright © 1983 by

Margaret Hatcher
University Press of America,™ Inc.

4720 Boston Way
Lanham, MD 20706

3 Henrietta Street
London WC2E 8LU England

Printed in the United States of America

Library of Congress Cataloging in Publication Data

Hatcher, Margaret.
    Centering through writing.

    1. Self-actualization (Psychology)   2. Laterality.
3. Creative writing.   I. Title.
BF637.S4H37   1983   158.1   83-14645
ISBN 0-8191-3449-X (alk. paper)
ISBN 0-8191-3450-3 (pbk. :   alk. paper)

DEDICATION

To all of my students--
who have been my best teachers.

To Charlotte--
for her confidence, support and love.

ACKNOWLEDGMENTS

Obviously, I am grateful to Janis Ross, my pottery instructor, for giving me the image of centering, but I am also indebted to other sources for inspiration and growth, the most important of which are some personal relationships which have encouraged, urged, lovingly pushed, given me permission and courage and safety to follow the path of centering in my life, in my art and in my teaching. Thank you, Charlotte, Ruffie and Martha.

Also, I am indebted to my students at the High School for Performing and Visual Arts who showed me what was meaningful to their growth, what worked and what didn't--and who had the trust in me and the strength in themselves to follow the path toward themselves. Credit and thanks should also be extended to my students whose work is reprinted in this book. All of these students were sophomores, juniors, or seniors in high school in the Creative Writing program I developed there. Not all of the work is revised or polished; none are perfect, but all were attempts at an authentic, honest expression of the inner and outer experiences that were meaningful to them. All were courageous steps toward the center of themselves as persons and writers.

My appreciation also extends to teachers who have shared with me their ideas, experiments, processes and approaches toward writing and teaching. Many of the suggestions, assignments, and approaches I offer in the book are by no means "my private property"--or perhaps even new to you. At this point, after sixteen years of teaching, I do not even know which were my ideas and which were given to me, much less by whom. Among the teachers of writing who have had the most significant influence on me and which I cite in this book are Ken MacCrorie, Jerome Judson, and Dalton McBee.

Also, my thanks and gratitude go to Dorothy Boswell for her suggestions which gave birth to the book, her insight and her careful typing of the early draft of the manuscript; to Norma Lowder, principal of HSPVA, for providing me with the support and opportunity to explore and develop a creative writing program that was a new approach to teaching writing; to Charlotte McGuire for her unswerving confidence in me and encouragement when I needed it most.

This book is written for both instructors and students of writing and for anyone who wants to use writing as a vehicle for centering right and left brain functions. I see the book as a guide and a source of motivation and stimulation rather than a strict program. I believe writing functions best when instructors and students alike work together as writers and audiences to explore, experiment, respond and offer advice. And I believe that in so doing, an atmosphere of trust, respect, and sharing develops which in itself is a part of the centering process.

TABLE OF CONTENTS

TABLE OF CONTENTS

TABLE OF CONTENTS

PREFACE

This book is about you--and me--and anyone who feels the need to live a more harmonious, creative, aware life, a more centered life. This book invites you into a process of centering, a series of experiences which lead you to discover your creative center through writing, a process by which you will develop your perception, imagination and insight.

The book itself is a product of the evolution of the centering process in me. Originally, I meant the book to be an educational text on creative writing for high school and college students. Only after the book was completed did I fully realize what the book meant or why the book screamed to be written. Only through working through the process of writing the book did I fully understand the process of that held it all together, the process of balancing right and left brain functions, the process of centering.

It struck me that the process I have been using to teach writing (a left brain function) has been a centering process, a way to bridge left and right brain functions, a process of <u>centering</u>, balancing. Basically, this book is written out of a feeling for and a belief in the centering process--the use of right brain functions to unlock the key to the left brain function of writing--and thus provide a medium by which each of us can become more balanced, centered, whole persons.

Writing is by no means the only process or even the "best" process for becoming centered; it is simply the one that I have had a great deal of success with, both as a teacher, a writer, and as a growing, creative, evolving person. As a tool for self-discovery, writing is invaluable. Each of us intuitively senses a universe flowing within us: a world of vaguely felt emotions and sensations; unexpressed ideas, perceptions, and awarenesses; unpainted canvasses of colors, textures, dreams, images, and real or imagined scenes; unwritten symphonies of word patterns, rhythms, melodies of thought. If we are unwilling to center on this rich universe flowing within us, it will become a blur of confused detail, a maze of awarenesses, impulses and superficial, external activity.

This book is written for the person who wants more than that blur and that maze. It is written for the person who seeks self-discovery, who wants to explore that universe flowing within, who wants to take those flowing sensations, those fleeting feelings and thoughts and form them into the reality of words written on paper to be structured and restructured, to be experienced and re-experienced, to be internalized until the words have a life of their own. This book is written for the person who is willing to use the key of centering to unlock the doors of the self, the heart, mind and the spirit, and to use the vehicle of writing to grow in self-awareness, self-renewal, harmony and--yes--the joy of creation.

CHAPTER I

THE CENTERING PROCESS: RIGHT BRAIN/LEFT BRAIN BALANCE

> One of the greatest tragedies of
> people's lives is that, in denying and
> repressing their inner emotional experience,
> they submerge in the underground of their
> unconscious not only their fear and their
> pain but their creative potential for the
> enjoyment of life.[1]
>
> --Nathaniel Branden

Agreed, but I feel the tragedy of our lives goes far beyond the denial and repression of our emotional experience: I believe we neglect and deny an entire world within us, a world that cannot be reached and known except through our desire to explore it, a world our western culture places little value in: the world of the right brain.

We are now in the early morning of our understanding of the latent, spectacular powers of the mind, the flexibility, power, and transcendence of which we are capable. However, brain/mind research of the past ten years has offered us conclusive evidence that the brain is our map and we ourselves are the great new frontier to be explored.

Neural Structure of the Brain

An exploration of the neural structure of the brain sheds some light on how we may best use this map that is our brain. Following is a simple and concise description of the circuitry of interconnecting elements (neurons or nerve cells) which make up the brain (see Illustration 1). Thinking is the outcome of the action of from ten to one hundred billion neurons constantly firing and exchanging information among themselves[2]. Each neuron consists of three major parts: dendrites, cell body (soma), and axon. The dendrites form the major receptacle surfaces of the neuron and are thus charged with conducting information (stimuli) from the neural field surrounding the neurons into the cell body where the information is coded and stored as an image. These images may be visual, tactile, audio, olfactorial or gustatorial. The more numerous, sensitive, and

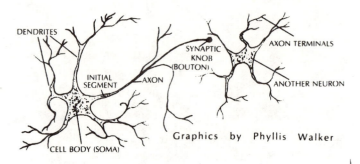

Graphics by Phyllis Walker

Illustration 1.

far-reaching these dendrites are, the greater their
capacity for receiving vast amounts of input.

Gaylean describes the neural process of
thinking in this way:

At the time that the stored information
is needed by the individual, cell salts of potas-
sium (+), chloride (-) and sodium (-) present
within the cell soma and surrounding neural
field intermix with each other through the
porous cell body membrane causing an increase in
the negativity of the intracellular cytoplasm,
thereby initiating an electrical charge
along the entire neural circuit. At that moment
the stored information exists from the cell body
along the axon and forms a quasi-juncture called
a synapse with a neighboring dendrite. All
information is transmitted via synaptic action,
thus scientists conclude that it is within the
synapse itself that knowledge takes place.
It is thought that one neuron, because
of expansive dendritic branching, can connect with as many as one thousand other neurons
at any given moment. The implications
for learning are astounding when mathematical
interpretations are applied to these data.
Ten to one hundred billion neurons interacting
with a thousand each at one time implies that the
brain is capable of processing from ten to one

hundred trillion bits of information in a lifetime. Since these are intuitive numbers, from a mathematical point of view, it seems that the brain's capacity for learning is infinite.[3]

Leonard reinforces the idea of the infinite capacity of the brain:

A brain composed of such neurons obviously can never be "filled up." Perhaps the more it knows, the more it can know and create. Perhaps, in fact, we can now propose an incredible hypothesis: <u>The ultimate creative capacity of the brain may be, for all practical purposes, infinite.</u>[4]

Gaylean points out that another significant factor to be explored is the process by which information is transmitted efficiently and smoothly throughout the circuitry of the brain's neurons:

The axons are coated with a fatty substance called myelin. Myelin is protected by a thin sheath of glia cells which also serve to regulate the cell salt balance between the cell body and surrounding neural field. Heavily myelinated axons conduct information more rapidly from the cell body than do less myelinated axons. Rusty wires are poor conductors of electricity, so to speak. Research on rats has shown that the production of myelin is heavily influenced by the presence or absence of two factors: <u>emotional closeness and enriched experiential learning environments.</u> Rats who were denied touch and affection by their keepers showed a significant dimunition in their production of myelin. In similar fashion, rats who were denied the opportunity of playing in complicated, maze-like labyrinths (representing enriched environments) also showed a dimunition in the production of myelin. On the other hand, an abundance of physical affection and the presence of learning tasks stimulated the production of myelin, and significantly improved dendritic and synaptic function. If we attempt a comparison with human cerebral functioning, the implications are clear. It

3

is possible that highly intelligent people have an abundance of healthy myelinated axons to assure the smooth and rapid transmission of vast amounts of information. If this is true, then <u>intelligence might possibly be nurtured through physical affection and enriched learning environments</u>. We know through experience that physical affection, the feeling of being wanted and valued, and enriched learning environments seem to facilitate the process of cognitive mastery. Brain research is increasing our empirical understanding of how crucial these two elements may be. It is well worth exploring the effects of using physical touch, affirmation strategies, and enriched, multi-sensory and complex problem solving activities. . . .[5]

Obviously, we are just on the brink of understanding the complexities and amazing capacities of our own minds; we are still struggling with what must be the most elusive frontier man has ever explored.

This book provides a step-by-step process for that exploration of the unknown universe of your own mind. This process is rooted in brain research and specifically in right-brain techniques which result in writing, a predominantly left-brain function. The result is a centering process, a balancing or bridging of the right and left hemispheres of the brain, a centering of the outer and inner worlds of self.

<u>Hemispheric Differentiation:</u>
<u>Right Brain/Left Brain Functions</u>

One of the most exciting and dramatic findings of brain/mind research is that the right and left cortical hemispheres of the brain have certain specialized, predictable functions and process information differently. One of the first to report this "split brain" phenomenon was Robert Ornstein in the <u>Scientific American</u> in 1967. Other research followed (Bogen, 1969; Kinsbourne, 1980; Ornstein, 1972; Wittrock, 1978) and verified the thesis of hemispheric differentiation.[6] By using brain scans of both cortices while subjects perform specific tasks such as daydreaming, counting, reading, writing or drawing, researchers have been able to determine the following specialized functions for the right and left brains:

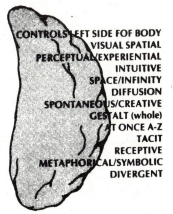

Left Brain   **Right Brain**

CONTROLS RIGHT SIDE OF BODY
VERBAL/NUMERICAL
LOGIC/LINEAR
INTELLECTUAL
CHRONOLOGICAL TIME
FOCUS
SEQUENTIAL
ANALYTIC (parts)
TRAIN OF THOUGHT A-B-C
EXPLICIT
ACTIVE
RATIONAL
CONVERGENT

CONTROLS LEFT SIDE FOF BODY
VISUAL SPATIAL
PERCEPTUAL/EXPERIENTIAL
INTUITIVE
SPACE/INFINITY
DIFFUSION
SPONTANEOUS/CREATIVE
GESTALT (whole)
AT ONCE A-Z
TACIT
RECEPTIVE
METAPHORICAL/SYMBOLIC
DIVERGENT

Illustration 2.

Although each hemisphere has the above
specialized functions, there is also a bilaterality
of the brain, meaning that each hemisphere also share
some functions and both participate in most activities.
The corpus callosum, a bundle of nerves and fibers
connecting the right and left cortices of the brain,
functions to allow information perceived by one side
of the brain to be received by the other. Without this,
our right hand literally would not know what our left
hand was doing.

In addition to specialized functions of the
right and left hemispheres, other findings emerging
from brain/mind research hold dramatic implications
for personal growth and increasing our intellectual
capacities. For example, we now know that the right
brain cannot verbalize what it knows; it is wordless,
speechless. Information in the right brain is stored
in images, senses, symbols and metaphors. The left
brain, on the other hand, must recognize and reformu-
late the images of the right brain into words before
information in the right brain can be communicated.
In short, the left brain is the "alphabet of the
mind."[7] The implications of that one fact alone are

5

far-reaching. Like the dream we vividly experienced in the night and which evaporated in the morning, unless we wrote it down as we dreamed it, the right brain world of intuitive, symbolic, holistic knowing is lost unless we capture it in words through the left brain.

Another significant finding relating to hemispheric differentiation is that, like a computer, the function of the left brain is to recognize, organize, and assimilate new information into already existing frameworks; its function is to recognize the relationship of stimulus to what it already knows. The left brain, in other words, is unable to create a meaning or generate new ideas. It is from the right brain that new ideas, total contexts, and creativity of meaning emerge. It is the right brain, then, which integrates novel, diffuse information and handles material for which there has been no previous experience. Hence, "without the right brain, there would be no idea; without the left brain, the idea would not be encoded, understood or communicated.[8]

These facts form the major premise on which this books rests: writing is a logical process by which we may become more directly connected to and familiar with the world of the right brain, and techniques which activate the right brain can be transferred to writing, a process which significantly enlivens and enpowers our writing. In short, it centers us.

Unfortunately, research indicates that our traditional educational system often emphasizes left hemispheric functioning to the neglect and even denial of right hemispheric acitivity.[9] Also, tests are designed to measure left brain analytical skills as the major determinant of IQ, and often the creative individual who perceives holistically rather than analytically is left little opportunity to achieve well on most IQ tests. Only recently has research begun to attach equal importance to right and left brain learning systems.[10]

Galyean's studies indicate that:

Traditional educational programs based on the tabula rasa concept of sequential acquisition of information work well for those with left hemispheric dominance, but for those who operate from a holistic and intuitive manner for processing information, prolonged

6

exposure to predominantly left hemispheric
learning strategies can severely hamper their
intellectual development. Many researchers even
believe that if certain right hemispheric
functions are not activated and used frequently
they will never fully develop.[11]

What has been happening in our traditional
western culture is reminiscent of the Sufi story about
Nasrudin:

A man saw Nasrudin on his knees searching
for something on the ground. "What have you
lost, Mulla?" he asked.
"My key," said Nasrudin.
So the man went down on his knees too and
they both looked and looked for the key. After
a time, the other man asked, "Where exactly
did you drop it?"
"In my house," answered Nasrudin.
"Then why are you looking for it here?"
"There's more light here than inside my
house," Nasrudin replied.[12]

Like Nasrudin, most of us tend to stay focused
on the place that has more light, on what is familiar
and easy, and in doing so, we neglect the place that
holds the key. The point, then, is not to neglect
the left brain in favor of the right, but let us not
neglect the right either, for it often holds the key
to the left.

The goal is to become equally familiar,
equally proficient in both modes. Ornstein notes:

Our highest creative achievements are
the product of the complementary functioning
of the two modes. Our intuitive knowledge
is never explicit, never precise in the scientific sense. It is only when the intellect
can begin to process the intuitive leaps, to
explain and "translate" the intuition into
operational and functional knowledge that
scientific understanding becomes complete.[13]

It is this ability to function equally well
in both modes which is at the heart of the centering
process and the "center" of the self-discovery process.

What is centering? Centering is a term that I
first encountered in yoga. Centering is feeling the
whole in every part, seeing the interrelatedness of
all parts that make the whole. It is the state of
openness, steadiness, intense concentration; it is
a time of peace, quiet, stillness, a time of harmony
and balance between the inner and outer worlds, a
time of focus and clarity.

I confronted the concept of centering again
when I took a pottery course. In potting, centering
is the process of bringing the clay into a spinning,
stable, unwobbling, focused whole by bringing it into
total balance at the center of the potter's wheel.
Centering is the first and the single most crucial
step in pottery, for it is centering which frees the
potter to mold the clay however he or she chooses.

An image that still is vivid in my mind is
important here: It is the image of Janis Ross, my
pottery teacher, sitting at her wheel demonstrating
how to center the clay. She was talking; her body was
so intensely focused on the clay that she did not need
to look at it. She was saying: "You cannot center the
clay without centering yourself . . . and by the way,
it took me years to learn to center the clay. . . ."
Her brilliant blue eyes were alive and bright . . . and
smiling. It was then that I understood why I often
have such agony and pain and frustration in writing
and painting and teaching and living . . . and sometimes why I have such beauty and joy and peace.

It was from these experiences with centering
that I fully understood my own process in writing, my
process in teaching writing, and the process of my
discovery of my own creative expressions--my poems, my
paintings, my life. The metaphor of centering the
clay in pottery seems a clear and appropriate means
of discussing centering through writing and the process
of balancing right and left hemispheres, for the
correspondences are extensive and relevant:[14] ***In
pottery, centering is the crucial step in forming
and transforming the clay from one shape to another,
from one texture (soft clay) to another (fired stone-
ware). In writing, centering is the step that opens
us up to the right brain functions of creating, transforming our experiences, sensations, desires, fears,

dreams, and thoughts into words, into a poem or story
that has a life and a shape of its own.   ***In
pottery, the center is always inward: it can be
reached only by bringing the outer world (left brain
functions) in balance with the inner world (right
brain functions). The potter does this by "talking
to" the clay with the hands, literally, by body
language, the touch of the hands on the spinning clay:
firm, tender, sensitive pressure, a touch which knows
when to yield, when to assert. Hands and clay press
against each other, both responding to the other to
come together, centered, whole, stable in an act of
merging the outer with the inner core of clay.

        To become centered persons, we must enter this
dialogue between ourselves as persons (the potter) and
our outer and inner experiences (the clay), the
materials from which we write and fashion stories and
poems. It is a dialogue conducted between the right
and left cortices: sense seeking sense, life seeking
life, innerness seeking outerness, awareness defining
awareness, perception seeking conception, transforma-
tion seeking its own growth. Centering--that sense
of quiet unity wherein we are confronted with all the
paradoxes and interrelated opposites, all the sensations, thoughts, experiences, emotions, intuition,
longings, insights into a fusion, a marging--and in
that dialogue we achieve a balance which enables us
as writers, like the potter, to mold and express perception into any shape we choose. ***To center the clay,
the potter must be steady and still, must concentrate,
listen through the hands to what the clay is whispering. The potter must be open to the clay, become
one with it, not separate, not fighting it or forcing
it.   In writing, we cannot separate ourselves from who
we are as persons. We must be steady and unwobbling
in the self-discovery, in the discovery of the wealth
of the world of the right brain, and in the discovery
of our creative center through writing. We must be
centered enough in ourselves to be open to all of our
experiences, both right and left, to all the rapture
and pain and beauty and chaos and potency. We must
be able to let it live in us and through us. It is
through that open awareness that we come to know ourselves and others through the writing we create out of
such feelings and experiences and moods. These crea-
tions are revelations of ourselves to ourselves. Our
poems are self-disclosures, the product of our own
perception and creativity, of our own center, our own
self.

These correspondences lead to a final realization: It is not the process of writing that is the point, although I thought it was at the outset of the book. It is the process of centering which is the point. It is ourselves, unfolding, growing, becoming centered, self-fulfilling, whole. This is the center of this book, to bring you into awareness of your own person, your own uniqueness, your own self and energy, your own separate experience, inner and outer, your own center. It is in and from this center that we create, that we transform ourselves from persons into poems and stories that we can share.

This book has a relish for the person and personal growth. The clay, before it is centered, is just a lump of dead stubborn clay; it has potential but that is all. This book offers a process of developing the potential of persons--in the art of writing, but more importantly, in the art of living, a process of in-depth experiencing, and in so experiencing, confirming the significance of who we are, what we have to say, and what it means to us.

I know that this is asking a great deal. I know that the centering process, the birth of self and person, is not without chaos and terror. I know it is a path that requires courage and perseverence, and that no amount of "awareness" can substitute for the daily work of the journey, simply putting one foot in front of the other on the path toward self. Centering and writing are stern disciplines, but rewarding ones. This book contains a process for beginning that discipline through writing. It doesn't profess to give all the answers by any means. But it does give a practical, step-by-step process for beginning the journey. Take one step at a time, put one foot, one perception, one word in front of the other, dawdle along the way if you wish--but do enjoy the path as you explore it. There is a person inside each of us who is constantly asking us to take this path toward ourselves, toward wholeness, who constantly seeks its center, as writer and as person. How do I know? Because you wouldn't have read this far, or have this book in your hands, if you had not heard that voice within. So listen to that self inside you, and follow--one step at a time.

FOOTNOTES: CHAPTER I

[1]Nathaniel Branden, The Psychology of Self-Esteem (New York: Viking Press, 1970), 8.

[2]The discussion dealing with neural structure of the brain is a summary based primarily on the following sources: Beverly Galyean, "The Brain, Intelligence and Education: Implications for Gifted Programs," Position Paper presented to the State Department of Education, Division of Gifted and Talented, January, 1981; Leslie Hart, How the Brain Works (New York: Basic Books, 1975); Carl Sagan, The Dragons of Eden (New York: Ballantine, 1977); Timothy Teyler, "The Brain Sciences: An Introduction," in Jeanne Chall and Alan Mirsky (eds.), Education and the Brain; The Seventy-Seventh Yearbook of the National Society for the Study of Education, Part 2 (Chicago, Illinois: University of Chicago Press, 1978), 1-32; Richard F. Thompson, Theodore W. Berger, and Stephen D. Berry, "Brain Anatomy and Function," in M. C. Wittrock (ed.), The Brain and Psychology (New York: Academic Press, 1980), 33-88.

[3]Galyean, 2.

[4]George Leonard, quoted in Marilyn Ferguson, The Brain Revolution (New York: Taplinger, 1973), 308.

[5]Galyean, 3-4.

[6]Basic sources used in the discussion of hemispheric differentiation: Robert Ornstein, The Psychology of Consciousness (New York: Viking Press, 1972); Joseph Bogen, "The Other Side of the Brain, I, II, III," Bulletin of the Los Angeles Neurological Studies (July, 1969); Marcel Kinsbourne, "Cognition and the Brain," in M. C. Wittrock (ed.), The Brain and Psychology (New York: Academic Press, 1980), 325-342; Marilyn Ferguson, The Brain Revolution (New York: Taplinger, 1973).

[7]Gaylean, 9.

[8]Beverly Galyean, "Using the Whole Brain," Tape (Long Beach, CA; KenZel, 1980).

[9]Bogen (1969); Marianne Frostig and Phyllis Maslow, "Neuropsychological Contributions to

11

Education," Journal of Learning Disabilities, 8 (October, 1978), 40-54; M. C. Wittrock, "Education and the Cognitive Processes of the Brain," in Jeanne Chall and Allan Mirsky (eds.), Education and the Brain, The Seventy-Seventh Yearbook of the National Society for the Study of Education, Part 2 (Chicago, Illinois: University of Chicago Press, 1978), 61-102.

[10]Such studies are: George Brown (ed.), Human Teaching for Human Learning (New York: Viking Press, 1971); Gaylean (1981); Robert E. Valett, Humanistic Education (St. Louis: C. V. Mosby Co., 1977); Gerald Weinstein and Mario Fantini, Toward Humanistic Education: A Curriculum of Affect (New York: Praeger, 1970).

[11]Galyean (1981), 10.

[12]Ornstein (1972), 187.

[13]Ornstein (1972), 12.

[14]The idea of using pottery as a metaphor for centering in the writing process was also influenced by M. C. Richard's book, Centering in Pottery, Poetry, and the Person (Middletown, Connecticut: Wesleyan University Press, 1962).

CHAPTER II

MULTI-SENSORY TECHNIQUES FOR CENTERING

In persons--in pottery--in poems--in
everything, the center is always inward. In the process of creating a space of peace and harmony in your
life, or of creating a poem, a story, or a clay pot,
that center can be reached only by bringing the outer
in balance with the inner. This means coming to your
senses, experiencing your outer world creatively,
imaginatively, perceptively, sensuously, fully.
Coming to your senses, literally, for a source of
fact/reality about your world is the first step in
centering. The physical senses--sight, sound, touch,
taste, and smell--are our primary sources of fact, a
sense of the isness/nowness/whatness of our outer
world of experience.

Marianne Moore applies the significance of
balancing the outer world of the senses with the
inner world of creativity in her poem below:

Poetry

I, too, dislike it;
There are things that are important beyond all
    this fiddle.
Reading it, however, with a perfect contempt for
    it,
        one discovers in it after all, a place
        for the genuine.
            Hands that can grasp, eyes
            that can dilate, hair that can rise
                if it must, these things are
                important not
            because a
high-sounding interpretation can be put upon them
but because they are useful. When they become so
derivative as to become unintelligible, the same
    thing may be said for all of us, that we
    do not admire what
  we cannot understand: the bat
                holding on upside down or in quest of
                something to eat,
        elephants pushing, a wild horse taking a roll
        a tireless world under a tree, the immovable
        critic
            twitching his skin like a horse that feels

13

                        a flea,
                    the baseball fan, the statistician--
                    nor is it valid to discriminate
                    against "business documents and
                        school books";
            All these are important. One must make a
                distinction however:
                    when dragged into prominence by half-poets,
                    the result is not poetry,
                        nor til the poets among us can be
                        "literalists of the imagination"--above
                    insolence and triviality and can present
                    for inspection, imaginary gardens with real
                        toads in them
                    shall he have it. In the meantime, if you
                        demand on the one hand,
                            the raw material in poetry in all its
                            rawness
                            and that which is on the other hand
                            genuine,
                            then you are interested in poetry.[1]

        We can create all the "imaginary gardens" we
wish, but until we observe with our senses fully alive,
until we re-experience with conscious awareness of
the "real toads" in those "imaginary gardens", we will
not fully know ourselves, and we will not be able to
take anyone with us on our trip; and worse, our
writing will simply bore the reader with all that
"fiddle." We must re-learn the skills of multi-
sensory knowing and observing that were natural to us
as a child, when we sensed the world was a wondrous
place, full of mystery and miracle, a world dreamed of,
anticipated with awe and excitement, a world not to be
missed or taken for granted.

Brain Research on Multi-Sensory Learning

        Through the use of brain scans, researchers
are now able to isolate the specific lobes and parts
of the brain which are primarily responsible for
certain types of mental activity and mental tasks.
Below is a diagram of the major lobes and areas of the
brain (see Illustration 3).

        Although there is interaction among all four
lobes of the brain, the temporal lobe has the primary
function of processing our senses of taste, hearing
and smell; the occipital lobe is the seat of visual
processing; the parietal lobe is responsible for the

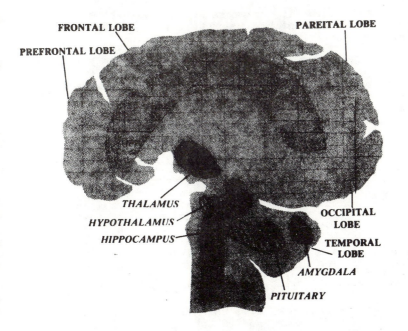

FRONTAL LOBE

PREFRONTAL LOBE

PAREITAL LOBE

THALAMUS

HYPOTHALAMUS

HIPPOCAMPUS

OCCIPITAL LOBE

TEMPORAL LOBE

AMYGDALA

PITUITARY

Illustration 3

body/mind connection, or the motor cortex, which provides the connection between the mind giving the body a command, and the body being able to process the command; and the <u>frontal lobe</u>, which is responsible for man's higher faculties. The frontal lobe is divided into two parts: 1) the prefrontal lobe, which is responsible for thinking, logical processing, abstraction, and creating, and 2) the frontal lobe, which is the seat of the higher values of life, such as the processing of love, friendship, global unity, beauty, joy, synergy of mind, mystical and spiritual knowing and transcendence. There is apparently a concomitant agreement and cooperation between the prefrontal and frontal lobes of the brain, so that "as we evolve with intelligence, we also evolve with the heart."[2]

Perhaps the key finding of research on the major lobes of the brain is that <u>brain scans prove that intelligence is directly related to multi-sensory processing.</u> In short, the more we can activate all

15

lobes simultaneously, the more we increase the chance
of retaining the information, the chance of whole
learning, centering.

Where do we begin, then, to recover this
natural multi-sensory awareness of the world within
and outside of us? One method is to return to that
state of natural curiosity and sensuality of the
child. A small child is by nature sensitive and sen-
suous, involved in sense play and exploration. Inno-
cense in a child can be said to mean "in-a-sense". To
a child, a bubble is a miracle, and though the child
does not know the word iridescence, he/she knows the
thing itself, for the bubble has taught the meaning.
The child does not have to be told or taught to
observe; the senses are alive and active, and the
child compulsively observes. A child may crawl on
hands and knees for an hour behind an ant, curiosity
impelling him/her to learn everything possible about
that marvelous creature. But then the child grows
older, and stops observing closely, and nothing seems
marvelous anymore; that natural curiosity dwindles.
The child is dying at age fifteen, though he/she may
not be buried for three or four score more years.

One reason we kill this natural sensuality is
that our social, moral and educational institutions
stress only one of our senses: sight. We condition
people to specialize, to become eye dominant. This
is reflected in our language: "seeing is believing,"
"see for yourself;" great men are called "seers" or
"visionaries," and when we leave someone, we say "see
you later," never taste, hear, smell or feel you
later, although those senses are every bit as active.

The problem with eye specialization is that
it tends to separate us from the world. I, separate
from the world, see differences. What would happen to
the racial conflicts if we were all blind?

Babies are biologically organized to be whole:
seeing, hearing, smelling, tasting, touching/feeling
. . . directly and naturally and without preference.
Babies are given five sense organs: eyes, ears, nose,
mouth and skin. BUT WE TEACH THEM NON-SENSE. At a
certain point we teach children to keep their hands
to themselves, not even to explore themselves. We
stop touching them. We teach they/learn to stay away
from one another, to keep our distance, to keep at
arm's length, to shake hands quickly and avoid real
contact. Thus we teach ourselves to ignore the

largest organ of the body: the skin. Sex is the only chance we really have to touch each other, and too often it is confined to touching of the so-called erogenous zones only.

In our ignorance of the other senses, we become imbalanced, tense, insensitive. Listening only to content instead of tone, rhythm, or pitch, we lose contact with the subtle messages of people and the world around us. We eat but do not really taste canned, frozen, artificially-flavored food: Is that why we have developed such bad taste? (Look at the blandness of most of our art, movies, architecture.) Smell has become such an odious word that whole industries are devoted expressly to its elimination.

Is it any wonder, then, that we have difficulty observing and sensing the real world around us and in us? Is it any wonder that we have difficulty centering within ourselves an outer world that we are not intimate with?

In some branches of the military services, part of the instruction consists of asking questions of a squad of men riding in an open truck. The instructor asks individuals such questions as "Was anyone at home in the last farmhouse? Does it have a telephone? Electricity? A basement? How many cows were in that pasture? Which direction were they facing? Why? Which direction is the wind coming from? About what is the wind velocity? In the third farmhouse back, were the windowshades up, down, or half-way up?"

In warfare, practice in observing such details may save lives. In peace, observation may not have such dramatic value, but it may add infinitely to the riches of our lives. Too many of us go through life with our senses so deadened that we function on a vegetable level. We plod unseeing, unhearing, unfeeling. One day is like all other days, one street like other streets, one joy like other joys, one face like other faces, caviar like hamburger, a rose no different than a sunflower. So we live and so we die, with death only a little unlike life, for in our living we noticed little to make the living different.

If this is the nature of most of your minutes and hours; if to you a puppy is only a young dog; if your nostrils send to your brain no message of pine

burning in a fireplace; if the noises of city streets
do not change subtly as the day wears on, if the old
newspaper vendor on the corner is merely an old man,
you especially will benefit from these exercises.

The habit of observing and sensing, like other
habits, must be developed and acquired through constant practice. Living fully, living awarely and
sensually, is like dying--no one can do it for you.
The exercises which follow will provide some techniques which will help you get into the habit of sensing
and observing again. They will teach you multi-sensory
whole knowing. In short, they will bring you to your
senses. However, these exercises can only provide a
starting place for you; the rest is up to you to
continue.

Visual Exercises

This first series of exercises is designed to
check your visual sense, your eyesight:

Exercise 1 - Zeroing In: Look around the room you are
in right now. What do you see when you look around
you right now? Look closely. Probably you see too
much--and not enough. Take a piece of paper and stick
a hole through it with the point of your pencil. Look
through the hole. Move the paper until you frame one
tiny part of your world--someone's hand, the print of
a girl's dress, the cracks in the wall. Now write a
thorough, specific, detailed description of what you
see.

Exercise 2 - A New Familiar Place: Go into a very
familiar room. Look at all the objects in great
detail . . . ONE AT A TIME. Experience each object
separately, for what it is. LOOK WITHOUT STARING.
Then see the room as a whole, from different angles,
from different points of view. What are its colors,
its nuances of light/dark/shadow? Selecting the most
important visual signs, paint the room with words;
give us its "feel" by letting us see it--through
your words.

Exercise 3 - The Missing Person: Pretend that you
are asked by the police to describe a missing person,
and that missing person is the person who was most
recently with you. Chances are that you know this
person well, so this exercise should be a cinch,

right? O.K., then list every specific detail about
that person--the exact color of the eyes (not hazel,
but gray-green, green-gray, purple), exactly what
clothes were worn, every detail you can think of about
the style of clothes, the color, the pattern of
clothing, the texture of the clothing. (If a shoelace
was frayed, which one was frayed?) How tall is this
person? Don't say about 5'6". Say 5'6½" if it is
about 5'6½". List weight, gestures, mannerisms,
anything that your eyes can see. Now, go to the
person, and read them your notes and compare it to
reality. Hmm . . . maybe not so easy as you thought?

Exercise 4: Now try to apply all your sharpened sense
of sight you have been developing in the preceding
exercises to this last exercise. This exercise is one
that is demanding, but always one which proves to be
very rewarding. Select a person in your life that
you have the opportunity to observe closely. You
should have a day or two of observation. Try to
observe that person in various activities, whether
it be at work, at home, at play. Take notes on what
you observe. At this point, do not be selective.
Take notes on every detail of physical appearance,
clothing, facial expressions, posture and gestures.
Especially give attention to any quality that seems
to you to be unique or characteristic of that person
and any clue that seems to be indicative of the
personality or character of that person. O.K., now
you are ready to look at all of the details and see if
they add up to any overall picture of that person.
Perhaps what they add up to is a very contradictory or
complex person, but try to make some generalization
on the basis of your details. Perhaps you will need
to select just a few of your details which seem to be
the most significant or interesting characteristics
about your subject. Perhaps the hands and the way
the person uses them tell you a great deal more about
the person that all the other clues put together, or
just the person's eyes, or the way they relate to
other people. You could describe the person doing a
uniquely typical action, such as laughing with friends
or sitting in a room doing some typical task. Whatever approach you choose to take, your task is to
share your visual image of your subject so specifically and so vividly that a reader will get a feel
for the person you are describing. Your description
may be written in poetry or in prose, whichever medium
seems most comfortable to you. It is hoped these

19

responses might give you some ideas for various
approaches and techniques you might want to try.

ON ALEX GEORGES

You're the big growly bear
With the stock broker manner
And nonchalant eyes
You're sure of what you do,
Your smile tells me that
But are you certain, bear,
That you're not on a chain?
Is that collar of confidence
A little too tight?
I think I've glimpsed you
Pulling against it.
All I know is
When your chain snaps,
I'm running for cover.

--Cathy Cain

SHE IS BEAUTIFUL

She is beautiful.
She stands hand on blue-jeaned hip,
    Marlboro in hand and tender mouth blowing
    smoke--
        not just smoking
    but looking cautiously, cat-like about as if
        threatened by
    everything around her.

She seems stuck here in life, not exactly sure of
        just which way
    to go, but going anyway, anywhere because there
        has to be a
    reason and place to go or else we wouldn't all
        be here going,
    right?

She is beautiful.
She stands there talking with her spider-like hands
        that grasp
        and throws messages out there for all of us
            to see.
        But we don't always look.
She smiles curious smiles when questioned,
    and laughs the answer back.
And just above these smiles are soft, wet eyes
    that look, and judge, pierce, and cry.

20

She is dance.
   She is art.
   She is play-acting.
She is cigarettes, and love, and anger all poured
 into one.
And did I say
That she is beautiful?
                        --Jerry Tipps
                          12th Grade

ON BRUCE VIEAUX

You pick up one of your assorted
pens and begin to
                print.
You never write but
                print.

And that printing unveils you . . .
each character
        rough and stiff and broad
-contradicts your obvious soft side -
      thus, the unveiling begins. . . .

      With that Chevy-Chase magnetism,
your pen spells out characters like

              you-
              your warm firm hands
              with soft warm clay
              mold and form to
              each grown, open hour.

      Yet, you hide. You hide behind
              the dark fuzz
              on the cheeks
      you build your own Great Wall to
peer over and to distill only as much
as is comfortable.

      You reach for your pen and write
                  honestly, openly
              but only once and
              you never revise.
      "What is said must be said
        and no costume jewelry
              allowed!"
That's what you write, but
that's what you aren't. . . .

21

```
              you aren't costume
                    ، jewelry,
              you're not side orders,
              you're not strangling
                         cellophane,
              you're not frozen
                         rain.
Although sometimes your eyes peek from
corner to corner suspiciously wandering,
you project yourself as solid,

              solid like Earth
              solid like Time
              solid as substance
                    that's what you are.
                         you are sustained, and
                              solid.

Solid as a 20th century Buddha.  You meditate
to me through your eyes; they translate
for you.

Sandwiched between a black head and
beard, your eyes stab outward and
conquer your world and mine too.

      You're not an outcast of society
   but you have rejected society,
                    it is your outcast.
                    It didn't fit your mold.
Again,
You pick up one of your assorted pens and
begin to print . . . with your
broad massive shoulders, like each
singly-printed letter, you stand alone
                              and solid.
                    --Suzanne Stroud
                    12th Grade
```

PROSE DESCRIPTION OF PHOEBE JEWELL

Her skin made the biggest impression on me
the first time I saw her. It has a look of
fragility and transparency, like baby-flesh. I
wanted to reach out and touch it, let my fingers
follow the soft curves of her face and trace the
outline of her faintly pouting lips.
      Her hair curls mellowly around her forehead
in relaxed curves that are repeated throughout

22

her face and body. Her face is pure and tranquil,
seemingly untouched with cosmetics but enhanced
by its own subtle palette of ashen pinks and
taupes. Then she looks up, forcing me to
re-evaluate. Those powerful green eyes shine
with friendliness and make her coloring glow
vividly on the smooth canvas of her face.

I see her mouth change often. When she is
not concentrating, the full upper lip barely
touches the brooding bend of the bottom one,
making her seem both vulnerable and compas-
sionate. The crests on her lips flatten,
the halves join together in a disciplined line,
and she begins to work.

She reminds me of a cherub when I look her
full in the face, but definitely a cherub with
a brain.

Her profile is classic, expressing the
Greek ideal of perfection, the balance of ten-
sions. Great strength of character shows in
the straight line of her nose and her firm
chin. This contrasts with the sloping lines of
her cheeks and neck, which show receptive femi-
ninity.

Her love for comfort is evident in the soft
clothing loosely encasing her body. It seems
that her body and mind must be free to do and
think as they please, with no restrictions.

When I look at her I think of liquids, not
solid matter, but also not insubstantial. I
taste the sweet tang of a full red wine, and
pull drenched material out of buckets of dark
dye. I look over Grecian oceans stretching out
into the immeasurable distance, seemingly clear
but hiding depth.

I'm watching her now, as she's doing her
assignment. Her left fist rests cushioned
against her cheekbone, balancing her head as she
reviews what she had just written. Her right
hand beats a slow, rhythmic tempo against the
desk top, impatiently pacing itself. She sits
up straight, clasping both hands captive in her
lap, to think and observe a moment. Then she
bends steadfastly over her paper, to begin
writing once again. The cherub is thinking
again.

--Charlie Moore
12th Grade

AFRAID OF THE DARK

You are the dark'side of the moon
There's a world back there somewhere,
But I never see it.
I can't explore it.
I haven't got the technology.
Once I saw a dim light;
It put a glow in the darkest point.
A greyness arose,
But it's black now.
I can't see.
The dark makes me nervous.

Your edges are bright.
But when I look a long time,
I notice shadows that have no form.
I can't tell what the shadows belong to
or where the light to make them comes from:
I only know that they're dark
And I can't explore them.

I'm afraid of the dark.

                    --Carol Lambert
                      10th Grade

Developing the Other Senses

        The point has been made that the other four
senses are often neglected and undeveloped because of
our dependence on our sense of sight. The activities
which follow should prove this point and should provide a starting place for correcting this imbalance.

        The general "rule" for all of the activities
which follow is that you must be blindfolded while
participating, or, if you can trust yourself not to
peek, you may just keep your eyes closed. This will
help you rely on your other senses and will clearly
show you how much you are dependent on your eyesight.

Exercise 5 - Orange A-Peeling: This exercise should
have a leader who will "talk" you through the activity.
The leader may be a friend, a family member, or anyone
with whom you feel comfortable and you trust to lead
you through the following steps: you will begin the
exercise with your eyes open, and you will have an
orange with you. Then, just follow the leader's
instructions: Take an orange in the palm of your hand.

See its shape, its color, its top and bottom, all of
the distinguishing marks on the skin. Do not rush
this process. Take all the time you need. Now, with
this visual image of your orange in mind, close your
eyes and do not open them again throughout the rest of
this exercise. As you are moving through this exercise, hold the visual image of the orange in your mind.
With your eyes closed, smell the orange. With your
fingernail you might want to puncture the skin of the
orange and note the difference in smell where it has
been punctured and where it is not. Smell the navel.
Does it smell different from the other parts of the
orange? Move the orange in the palm of your hands.
Listen closely to the sound your hands make in contacting it. Experiment with different sounds your
hands can make against the orange. Now, roll the
orange over the surface of your face. Notice the difference in the way it feels on different parts of your
face. Keeping your eyes closed, feel the temperature
of the orange on your face, the texture. Experience
how your face feels. Now, open your eyes and look
at the orange again. Do you see it differently? Do
you see it better? Very gently and sensitively break
the skin and begin to very slowly pull the skin away
from the meat of the orange. See the juice come out
of the skin. Feel the juice. Hear the sounds the
skin makes as it pulls away from the meat of the
orange. Do it so slowly that you can watch it pull
and tear apart. See if you can keep the skin together
so it comes off in one large piece. Take your time.
Listen to the sounds. Experience every sense of the
orange, as if you have never seen an orange before,
as if you have never peeled an orange before. Look at
the flesh of the orange. Feel it. Now, as slowly as
you can, break the orange in half and separate its
quarters. Tear off one section at a time. Again, do
this very slowly and as gently as you can. Note the
difference in sounds and the way the skin adheres
between sections. Now close your eyes again and eat
the orange one section at a time. Try to experience
the feel of it in your mouth as well as its smell, and
expecially try to eat each section in a different way
from all the other sections. Be as creative as you
can, experiment as much as you can with each section.
Enjoy.

Exercise 6 - The Blind Shower: This is an exercise
which you will probably do in private and at your
home. If you prefer a bath to a shower, just make
the necessary adjustments. Here are your instructions:

Adjust the water temperature in your shower, then step into the shower and close your eyes. Keep your eyes closed. Experience the water on your skin. Experience the texture, the flow, the temperature and experiment how each feels on different parts of your body. Be very attuned to the sounds and smells in the shower. Shampoo your hair and experience all of the sensations--water, soap, soapy hair, soap sliding down your skin, everything. Keeping your eyes closed, soap your whole body slowly. Experience it all. Then write the experience down in as much detail as you possibly can, after your shower.

Exercise 7: The following exercises work better and are more fun in a group setting--or at least with a partner. Basically they are exercises to test your accuracy and observation levels in your senses of feel, smell, taste, and sound:

Feelies--Collect several objects of differing sizes, weights and textures. The purpose of this exercise is to see who can identify the objects by just feeling them--no peeking or smelling or hearing or tasting the objects is allowed. This can be made into a game, using a variation of a "spelling bee" or "relay" approach.

Smellies--You can test your sense of smell by much the same procedure as the "feelies" exercise, using coffee, mustard, horseradish, mud, and so forth, or by mixing any number of odors or fragrances. The best noses will be able to recognize two or more odors that have been mixed together.

Tasties--You guessed it, another exercise like those above, but this time, you must hold your nose, as well as close your eyes, and identify different tastes, such as various brands of soft drinks, candy bars, spices, and so forth, by taste alone. Did you do better? Hummmmm, a very interesting game--especially right before lunch break!

Hearies--Now collect sounds--the crunch of paper, the rustle of silk, the clink of coins, or perhaps something more complicated, as the sound of an oboe or the twang of a violin string or even a sound effects record. See how many sounds each person can recognize.

Exercise 8 - Writing Without Words: Let's do some creative work with your sense of sound. Using a sound effects record, or any series of sound clues you can create, tape record sounds which tell a story, a

26

sequence of events. For example, if you translated these words into sounds, could you imagine the scene of what is happening?

> Arf! Arf! Arf!
> Scratch, scratch!
> Woof! Woof!
> Footsteps
> Click
> Squeak
> Patter, patter, patter.

Sounds like a dog being let into the house, doesn't it? Now, you try it. Compose a story or scenario by using sounds only. The first step is to outline the events in the scenario or story that rely heavily on sounds. No dialogue is allowed. Next cut the story to sounds only. This demands that you concentrate on all the sounds around you and that you become acutely aware of how suggestive various sounds are. If you have the equipment, record your soundtrack on a cassette, play your tape for your classmates or friends and have them narrate the story as they hear it.

Exercise 9 - Personal Universe: Here are two variations of the same exercise, both of which are designed to increase your knowledge of your senses as they relate to your own body and your own space. For both exercises, you will need a leader to talk you through the exercise. The scripts the leader should follow are below.[3]

Find your own space somewhere in the room and occupy it. Close your eyes. Feel the space around you and try to get a picture of the shape and area of your space. You are in an envelope of space which moves with you. Make yourself comfortable in your space. Now, concentrating only on your sense of touch, discover as many textures about yourself as you can. (Give about two minutes for this.) Continue to discover even more undiscovered textures. (Give another minute.) Relax. Now tune in to your sense of smell to the exclusion of all other senses. How do different parts of your body smell. (Allow about one minute.) Now attend only to taste. How great a variety of tastes about you can you discover? (Allow a minute.) Relax. Now listen to the sounds of yourself; at some point put your hands over your ears. Can you hear your blood moving, your heart beating, any noises about your body? Relax. Look around the room. Now choose a partner. Go with your partner to your space. Share with each other the senses as in the previous exercise. Share with your partner the single most outstanding impression you have of him as a result of this experience. Though it can be too threatening to some groups to taste partners, an interesting alternative is to have each person tell his partner what he thinks he would taste like.

Variation B: Sit again in a large circle. Face toward the wall and get into your most secure position. Feel your space around you. For the next fifty years you cannot move your body and your space will be your universe. Begin to explore your universe. (Allow at least three minutes for this exploration.) If you choose, let the sounds come out which are characteristic of your universe. Let the sounds become louder. Start to emerge from your universe. Return to the circle. Share experiences with others.

When I first performed this exercise, I soon realized that even without moving or seeing, my universe was quite extensive and fascinating, and I had enough things to interest me for perhaps a few years. For instance, just exploring my teeth with my tongue could occupy me for a day or so. Getting into an itch was quite an experience. The sounds of the world around me became amplified and were very inter- esting. The sounds that we emitted, those of our own personal universe, were a fascinating mixture of almost supernatural and deeply emotional utterances.

Exercise 10 - A Trip Through Your Senses: For this exercise, you will need a partner and a blindfold. This is an exercise in sensing, and you must trust your partner to lead you through a sense-full trip, a variety of sounds, textures, smells, and wherever appropriate, tastes. Also, since you will be blind- folded, you will have to trust your partner with your safe movement through space and the senses; in other words, you will learn to trust communication by touch. After you have selected your partner, you will deter- mine who will act as guide and who will be blindfolded first. The guide's role is: (1) to communicate with your partner by touch, such as where to walk, stop, turn, step up, step down, and so forth. In short, the guide is to make the partner feel secure, even without eyesight; (2) to direct your partner on a journey which would provide a variety of smells, sounds textures and tastes; (3) to maintain a flow of dialogue with your partner concerning what he is sensing--ask, then give clues, then tell your partner how accurate/ inaccurate his perceptions are. After a trip of about 20 minutes, the partners should exchange roles--the

guide dons the blindfold, the traveler becomes the
guide. Some surprises are in store for you, especially if you enjoy a childlike sense of mystery and
adventure of the senses!

Exercise 11 - To Touch or Be Touched: This activity
is very difficult for some people and must be handled
with care and sensitivity by all who wish to participate. Also, it should be understood at the outset
that no one should feel forced to participate in this
particular exercise. This is an exercise in touching--
experiencing the sensation of being touched by different people in different ways, and in touching
others in a variety of ways. Because our society and
culture teach us not to touch one another, except
for occasional "safe" handclasps and pats on the back,
or when we are given permission to touch one another in
sexual relationships, most of us feel somewhat uncomfortable touching or being touched. And yet, there is
abundant evidence that touching is healing, a vehicle
of balancing our inner and outer worlds, of centering.
This exercise will teach you a great deal about how
comfortable you are in using your largest sense
organ--your skin.
        You should have two groups--the "touchers"
and the "touchees", for lack of better terms. The
touchees are seated, blindfolded in a tight circle
facing inside the circle. The touchers stand outside
the circle, one toucher behind each touchee.
        It is very important that everyone understand
that the exercise be conducted in complete silence,
for the value of the exercise comes from concentration
on what each person is communicating to the other
through the sense of touch. Any comments or noise
will be distracting and will break the mood and concentration.
        The touchers should attempt to give each
person a variety of sensations through exploring
different areas of the body being touched. The
touchers should be considerate of the areas that are
socially off-limits or which might be ticklish or
sensitive. Also, the touchers should try to experiment
with different types of touches--massaging, patting,
light touches, tapping, squeezing, and so forth.
        The touchees should simply try to relax, to
be totally trusting and passive, and to simply experience and be aware of the various sensations they are
receiving.
        The touchers should rotate around the circle,
touching one person for about two minutes, then at a

29

non-verbal signal from a leader, everyone should move 1 another person.

After about 15 minutes, or when each toucher has touched at least five different people, roles should be reversed: touchers become touchees, and vice-versa.

After the exercise, verbalize your feelings and sensations in writing. What did you like? What didn't you like? What was most pleasant? What made you uncomfortable? What was surprising? What made you self-conscious? Could you tell who was tense? What subtle signals communicated emotions to you? What have you learned about yourself through this exercise?

Exercise 12 - As If for the First Time--or Five Minutes of Beauty A Day:[4] It seems only fitting to end this section of exploring and sharpening our senses with this exercise. It should serve as a reward--as well as a reminder for you to keep working at being aware of and using your senses--all of them--daily.

This exercise is really a recipe for experiencing beauty--and as a result, pleasure. When you can do this exercise for even a few seconds, you will realize an extraordinary sense of release and freedom. The more artificial, hurried and graceless your life is, the more you will benefit from this experience.

You should set aside five minutes a day for this exercise. Do you have that much time to experience the beauty of the world around you? When was the last time you did that--consciously, fully, completely?

Beauty starvation is almost as widespread as love starvation. Often we simply do not realize what we are starving for. In our world of traffic jams and plastic flowers and concrete, we are so far removed from the pure experiences of our senses that we do not even realize our senses have become deadened.

Before we get into what, specifically, this exercise requires of you, let's talk about one thing it asks you NOT to do: It requires that you are NOT to think, NOT to describe, NOT to compare. It asks you NOT to be conscious at all of words. Drop them, lose them, leave them behind in your journal or with your teachers at school. Just enter the world of pure sensation.

Here is the recipe: First, select any kind of beauty you prefer, or any kind of beauty to find around you, providing that it is a natural beauty. Choose a beauty outside yourself, not one which may be within you, in your memory or imagination. We will use that later.

Next, give your attention to only one sense: taste only--touch only--see only--hear only--smell only. If more than one sense makes its way to you, do not willfully keep it out of your consciousness, but do not give it your attention either; simply let it be. Fix your attention on the one sense you have chosen. For example, choose a taste, the taste of an apple. Bite into the apple. Taste it, without thinking about any other apple bite you ever experienced. Simply taste the appleness of that apple. Or if you choose to feel beauty through touch, only touch. Do not move your hands; leave your hand on what you are touching--and receive.

This exercise is 3000 years old. It was given by Shiva to the Goddess Parvati. Shiva said, "Radiant One, see as if for the first time a beauteous person or an ordinary object." As if for the first time-- this is the essence--this is the lesson for coming to our senses, of knowing with all senses, with all lobes of the brain.

FOOTNOTES: CHAPTER II

[1]Marianne Moore, "Poetry," _Poetry is for People_, Martha McDonough and William C. Doster (eds.) (Boston: Allyn and Bacon, Inc., 1965), 5-6.

[2]Beverly Gaylean, "Using the Whole Brain," Tape (Long Beach, CA: KenZel, 1980).

[3]Script adapted from "Education of Self," exercises in Harold C. Lyon, _Learning to Feel--Feeling to Learn_ (Columbus, OH: Charles E. Merrill Publishing Co., 1971), 134-35.

[4]An adaptation of "As If for the First Time," in Laura A. Huxley, _You Are Not the Target_ (North Hollywood, CA: Wilshire Book Co., 1963), 156-59.

CHAPTER III

BRIDGING TECHNIQUES:
TURNING THE SENSES INTO CONCEPTS

Now, let's assume that the preceding chapter is beginning to work for you, that you are becoming more and more aware of, and in tune to, your senses--that you are coming to your senses--all of them. Wonderful! Feels good, doesn't it, to be alive and sensitized to the world around you?

Then let's go a step further on that trip into your senses, your world of the right brain. How do you "make sense" out of all this sense awareness? How do you communicate it to someone else? How do you turn the senses into concepts? Unfortunately, it doesn't just magically happen--at least not for most of us! It happens by bridging right and left brain functions, and the result may be music, or art, or words in the form of a poem, story, play or essay.

Remember in Chapter I, the specialized functions of right and left brain were discussed. If you recall, the left brain specializes in the verbal, logical, conceptual thinking processes. This chapter will deal with exercises and techniques which teach you to bridge or translate the senses, the perceptual knowing of the right brain into the language of the left brain--words, so that the rich world of the right brain can be shared in a way others can understand. First, though, a distinction must be made between sensing/observing and thinking.

Perceptual and Conceptual Thinking

Perceptual thinking is thinking in images and senses: it is a kind of thinking that does not require words. Literally, the verb to perceive means to take through the senses. When you performed the "Orange-A-Peeling" exercise, you were doing perceptual thinking guided by what your senses were taking in: no words at all were necessary for you to do that exercise. Now, picture in your mind what you ate for supper last night. Remember the taste and texture of the food in your mouth. When you picture in your mind events and objects and experiences which aren't present, you are doing perceptual thinking based on what your senses have taken in in the past.

Suppose, however, that instead of peeling and eating the orange, you need to tell someone how to do it. Perhaps in a simple case, showing might work, but probably your percepts, or senses, would need expression, would need words, to be fully comprehensible.

Conceptual thinking is thinking with words. Words are simply symbols that stand for concepts which express our understanding about what we perceive. Here is an example:

Consider the word between. In order to understand the concept represented by between you must have had experiences in which you perceived pairs of objects and then focused on the space that separated them. That, in turn, implies that you were able to pick pairs of objects out of a random collection. When you could readily isolate pairs of objects, you could then think about their relationships to one another--for instance, about the space around them and about a point to the left or right or between them. Finally, you were able to talk and think about the relationships of pairs of objects and the spaces around and between them without actually having the objects present. You then fully understood the concept of between.[1]

From Percepts to Concepts

Generally, psychologists and linguists agree that most concepts develop after and from perceptual experiences. Concepts are both built from and triggered by percepts, and there is, in fact, a point at which perceptual thinking and conceptual thinking seem almost to occur simultaneously. That is a point of centeredness. The following exercise should illustrate this point.

Exercise 1: Gather together several musical instruments, such as a flute, guitar, violin, saxophone, and oboe. If you do not have access to musical instruments to illustrate the sounds "live", listen to

recordings which spotlight different instruments.
First, simply perceive the sounds; experience the
difference in tonality, pitch and timbre through your
senses. Note that you need no words to "sense" similarities and differences. However, as you listen,
it is quite probable that words, hence, concepts, such
as same, higher, softer, and other comparative words
occurred to you. Right? The between-ness of sensing
must be verbalized because it is a concept.

Did this exercise illustrate that there is no
simple way to decide where perceptual thinking ends
and conceptual thinking begins? All right, then,
let's not worry too much about separating perceptual
and conceptual thinking: let's work on making better
use of them by accepting that our concepts are clari-
fied and made real to others by our ability to translate our world of thought into a world of the senses
that is bridging, the act of centering right and left
hemispheres of the brain.

Below are a series of exercises and writing
assignments which will give you practice in going from
percepts (senses) to concepts (words): in short, in
turning senses into words.

Exercise 2 - Getting Sensitized to Sense Words:

Step 1. Select a basic color--blue, for
example. Look around you and jot down all the words
you would use to describe the different blues you see
right now. Try to name the specific shade of blue each
object has. Do you have enough words to really be
accurate? It is O.K. to argue with yourself--I mean,
you'll still be the winner, right? It's a contest
with yourself. How many ways can you describe the different shades of blue you see right now? Go ahead--it
is blue, isn't it? Well, is it navy blue? Amethyst?
Turquoise? Cerulean?
This can be frustrating, but also intriguing
to recognize that our eyes have a language, a recog-
nition of subtle differences, that perhaps our
vocabulary is too limited to express. So let's go
another step.

Step 2. Compile a list of sense words. Here
are the ground rules:

a) Your sense word list will be divided into
   five categories: 1) color and visual
   qualities; 2) pattern and shape; 3) touch
   and texture; 4) sound; and 5) smell.

b) The words may be adjectives or nouns only.
c) No hyphenated or double words (such as off-white, deep purple) may be used.
d) No trade-name colors may be used.
e) Only one form of a word per category is permitted.
f) You may want to use words you are already aware of and sensitive to, then you may want to add to the list words you find by consulting dictionaries, paint sets, friends and other sources.

Step 3. Hopefully, the result of compiling this list is that you recognize the wealth of sense words available in our language. Use your list as a guide and a resource. Below is a sample list. These are by no means all the words that could be included on these lists, of course, but this might contain some words not included in yours:

SOUNDS

ringing	cheeping	gasping	smashing
piercing	peeping	whooping	tinkling
raucous	chittering	crooning	bellowing
tolling	clucking	silent	tapping
soothing	crowing	tranquil	melody
cacophony	singing	quiet	tune
loud	tinkling	noisy	rhythm
mumbling	twittering	din	beat
blaring	cawing	racket	chattering
whispering	mewing	snapping	snoring
yelling	mooing	crackling	sighing
screaming	lowing	banging	wailing
screeching	oinking	thunderous	scratching
bellering	snorting	crashing	crunching
shouting	cooing	ripping	bubbling
rumbling	sneezing	swishing	fizzing
honking	wheezing	buzzing	snivelling
quacking	whining	hissing	bawling
trumpeting	coughing	pealing	rattling
grunting	barking	clanging	tone
squealing	howling	splashing	volume
moaning	yipping	rustling	pitch
keening	yapping	clattering	croaking
crying	growling	thumping	burping
sobbing	snarling	bumping	gagging
chirping			

TOTAL: 101 words

TOUCH AND TEXTURE

rough	stubbly	fiery	bushy
shaggy	slick	lacy	tangled
spiky	slippery	creamy	matted
splintered	slimy	curdled	greasy
corduroy	icy	waxy	coarse
grainy	cold	metallic	fine
smooth	freezing	steely	keen
velvety	numbing	ivory	sharp
silky	piercing	rutted	biting
glassy	cool	grooved	bubbly
shiny	warm	inlaid	soapy
polished	hot	engraved	gritty
sheen	scalding	stinging	sandy
sheer	boiling	bumpy	rocky
fuzzy	searing	fluffy	cushioned
furry	scorching	cottony	soft
hairy	burning	wooly	hard
foamy	dank	patina	gripped
glossy	wet	pocked	tweedy
matte	moist	scarred	kiss
pulpy	clammy	prickly	rasping
grimy	sopping	itching	abrasive
dusty	scaled	scratchy	chapped
dirty	downy	corrugated	raw
damp	fluted	tickling	sculptured
dry	knobbed	pressed	

TOTAL: 103 words

COLOR AND VISUAL QUALITIES

red	saffron	bright	dark
scarlet	gold	dull	light
carnelian	silver	rose	chocolate
crimson	chrome	lilac	sienna
vermilion	copper	lime	salmon
yellow	bronze	avocado	coral
lemon	purple	pale	primrose
canary	violet	ashen	cerise
topaz	mahogany	ruddy	gamboge
blue	ebony	flushed	maroon
amethyst	crystalline	cyan	amber
navy	wine	white	poppy

cobalt	burgundy	olive	fuchsia
turquoise	claret	drab	chartreuse
black	clear	brilliant	orchid
obsidian	transparent	khaki	opaque
jet	glassy	lavendar	translucent
gray	rust	carmine	sapphire
dun	cordovan	indigo	milky
tan	grizzly	ocher	flesh
buff	brindle	umber	peach
chestnut	snowy	ultramarine	mustard
green	smoke	sepia	mint
aqua	pearl or pearly	walnut	brass
aquamarine	ivory	henna	citrine
orange	cream	azure	onyx
pink	mauve	sable	jade
puce	spruce	slate	garnet
magenta	iridescent	lake	maize
ruby	shimmering	plum	charcoal
emerald	twinkling	bistre	sooty

TOTAL: 124 words

SMELL

perfumed	lilac	earthy	stinking
scent	lemon	loamy	fetid
odor	fragrance	sweaty	sharp
rose	lime	rotten	biting
pungent	musky	plastic	acrid
spicy	mildewed	fishy	flowery
acid	moldy	doggy	nauseating
alkaline	dirty	skunky	redolent
sulphurous	piney	beery	vinegary
stale	sweet	tart	minty
fresh	sour	putrid	moist
musty	spoiled		

TOTAL: 46 words

PATTERN AND SHAPE

round	parallel	narrow	reticulated
circular	angular	wide	crested
spherical	flat	deep	eyed
globe	rounded	shallow	drooping
orb	rolling	dappled	erect
hemisphere	curved	pied	concentric
ball	shapely	checkered	adjacent
triangle	sharp	short	depressed
pyramid	concave	long	swollen
cone	convex	streamlined	sunken
square	diagonal	contoured	protruding
rectangle	horizontal	terrain	banded
cube	vertical	aquiline	veined
cylinder	depth	disc	palmate
box	width	plate	pinnate
arc	height	thread	spiked
elliptical	length	wormlike	crowned
crescent	girth	serpentine	cupped
pentagon	breadth	sinuous	baggy
oval	spotted	winding	tight
hexagon	brindled	waved	loose
octagon	striped	kinky	spiral
tetrahedron	solid	lanky	corkscrewed
polyhedron	frail	curly	helix
trapezoid	thin	crystalline	fanned
ovate	plump	pointed	paisley
ellipsoidal			

TOTAL: 105 words

It is interesting to note that the list of smells is by far the shortest. Was yours? Any ideas why this may be? Psychologists have observed that, although odor is important to us and has strong emotional effects on us, it is our least developed sense.

Exercise 3 - Sense Collage: As a follow-up to your sense word list, choose a word and make a collage or poster to illustrate it. In your collage use as many shapes, colors, forms, patterns and textures as you can. Don't rely too much on magazine pictures; if you can find a snail shell, don't use a picture of one in your collage. You might take the word "spiral" from the word list. Think of all the spiral forms in nature, not to mention geometric shapes, foods and textures that are spiral, and then put it together in a collage. In other words, in your collage, try to visualize every sensory association with that word by appealing to and including every sense response you can. Talk about a trip through your senses!

Exercise 4 - Color Poems: Now that you've made some effort to find words to fit subtle variations in the senses, let's try to put those words into poetry, and let's just go back to color. Let's write some color poems.

Step 1. Select your favorite color. If you have more than one, or if your favorite color depends on the mood or situation you are in, simply choose the color that seems most appropriate to you at this moment.

Step 2. Develop a color log by using the following questions as a means of collecting associated words, images, memories and ideas:

a) What words describe this color or some shade of it? There may be one word or there may be ten or 12 words. List all of those words used to describe this color.
b) What objects in nature are this color? What other objects are this color?
c) What mood do you associate with the color? Why?
d) What personal memories are associated with the color?
e) How might the color be expressed in terms of sound, smell, taste, and touch? For example, if red were expressed in music, how might it sound? How would purple taste? How would yellow feel to touch? Allow yourself several days to "walk around" with your color, to really "get into" the feel and taste and touch and smell of it, become that color, but especially delve into your associations and memories related to it.

Step 3. Meanwhile, read some poems professional poets have written out of their associations with color. A good source of color poems is Mary O'Neill's Hailstones and Halibut Bones. If that book isn't available, here are a few color poems that are interesting:

EARLY MORNING: CAPE COD

We wake to double blue
An ocean without a sail,
Sky without a clue
Off white
Morning is a veil
Sewn of only two
Threads, one pale,
One bright.

We bathe as if in ink,
But peacock-eyes and clear;
A roof of periwink
Goes steep
Into a bell of air
Vacant to the brink.
Far as we can peer
Is deep
Royal blue and sky
Iris, queen and king
Colors of low
And high.
And now across our gaze
A snowy hull
Appears:
Triangles
Along its stays
Break out to windpulls.

With creaking shears
The bright
Gulls cut the veil
In two,
And many a clue
On scalloped sail
Dots with white
Our double blue.

--May Swenson[2]

UNDER THE HARVEST MOON

Under the harvest moon,
When the soft silver
Drys shimmering
Over the garden nights,
Death, the gray mocker,
Comes and whispers to you
As a beautiful friend
Who remembers
Under the summer roses
When the fragrant crimson
Lurks in the dusk
Of the wild red leaves,
Love, with little hands,
Comes and touches you
With a thousand crimson memories
And asks you
Beautiful, unanswerable questions.

--Carl Sandburg[3]

41

SYMPHONY IN YELLOW

An omnibus across the bridge
    Crawls like a yellow butterfly,
    And, here and there, a passer-by
Shows like a little restless midge.

Big barges full of yellow hay
    Are moored against the shadowy wharf
    And like a yellow silken scarf
The thick fog hangs along the quay.

The yellow leaves begin to fade
    And flutter from the terrible elms,
    And at my feet the pale green Thames
Lies like a rod of rippled jade.

            --Oscar Wilde[4]

Step 4. Which of these poems do you think uses color most effectively? Keep in mind that although each uses color as a controlling image, each of the three poems uses it to different effect and for different purposes. For example, which poem uses color primarily to paint a picture, to let you see it the way the poet sees it? Which uses color in order to express a memory? To make a statement? Which relies more on metaphor and simile in expressing color?

Step 5. Now you are ready to try it! Drawing ideas from your color log, and using suggestions from your study of the preceding models, write a piece suggested by memories, senses and images which you associate with your favorite color. Remember, you can't use everything you wrote in your color log, but that is a place to start. See what in your color log interests you and most strongly makes you feel the emotion of the color.

If you are totally stumped and have no ideas on how to get started, below are some suggestions. Just insert a color in the blank and try free association technicolor:

    a) Dreaming in _____.
    b) A _____ afternoon (morning, evening)
    c) _____ reveries.

    d) A _____ future.

Step 6. Good! You've written a color poem, at least a first draft! How did that feel? After you've finished your first draft, these guidelines might be helpful for revision:

a) Is the sketch unified around a central idea related to color? Is this central idea clear? Do all details contribute to it?
b) Are sharp, well-chosen, accurate words used to create vivid, sharp pictures? Are the images fresh? Interesting?
c) Is figurative language used to tell what the color is like, in terms of the senses?
d) Is the piece interesting, alive, original? How could it be more so?
e) Does the structure and word choice fit the meaning?
f) As a final touch, you might want to mount your final copy on construction paper of the appropriate color. (I mean--really--it takes just a bit more to go first class!)

Below are some samples of student poems written in response to this assignment. Remember: If these students can do it, so can you!

EVENING POETICS

```
Evening breathes lavender
                    into
                my years--
          purple pasts
               of
          poets' dreams.
And I
     on magenta couch
                    lie
                    and
                         view
          with amethyst eyes
               Wilde
                    in lace and lilac
But behind the drapes
                    of plum and gold
          Eliot paces--
                    looks to the sky
An orchid film
          streaks the air
                    shimmers
                         darkens
          and waits
                    for violet.
          So do I.
```

                              --Martha Brown
                               12th Grade

43

On either side press banks of green
Above is blue and white patch sky
The violet highway sings between

--Marion Weaver
12th Grade

The white met the blue--
There washed, there mixed:
At the churning-point our reds yellow browns
Laid a bracelet-chain along the beach.

--Marion Weaver
12th Grade

Trees with smoke limbs
Slept under a stone-staring murmur.
Sky like a steel pan lay across the rooftops.
The river was a winding bar of lead.
And across the street--a bright black cat ran.

--Marion Weaver
12th Grade

Exercise 5 - Sense Piece: Now follow the same process
that you did with the color poem, but do it with any
of the five senses in prose or poetry. Select a
sound--or a texture--or a smell--and go with it! Firs
develop the sense log, then try to develop a finished
written piece of that. Again, you might wish to build
the piece around an experience or memory associated
with that particular sense, or you might deal with it
in a purely descriptive way, or through image, metaphor or simile. But remember, the exercise here is to
be as specific as possible with the senses, in
observing as well as expressing what you observe in
words.

Here are some student pieces to use as models
for this exercise. First is a poem which concentrates
on the texture of sand to describe a kind of person.

SANDSTORM

Seeing your world through a sandstorm
All is blurred, and scratchy,
Like a warped record.
Grains of sand strike your eyes,
Bringing tears--
You wipe them away, and walk on.
Battered by angry winds
That blasted all of your thick skin away,
Leaving you raw, and naked;

44

You coated yourself with their grains,
Layers and layers.
You are sand-paper rough,
Sand-paper tough,
And you scratch.
Your ears are full of sand--
You hear only the ceaseless grinding.
Your mouth, too, is full of sand--
You spit out some, swallow more,
And cannot taste--
Not the bloody smoke
Nor the Hollywood laughter
Nor the sunshine
Winding its way
Through tall trees.
Only sand
And more sand--
You are wrapped up in sand
Till you can't move, can't think
Can't feel.
You are the sand--
You are the storm.

                    --Juliet Lee
                      10th Grade

The following poems take the sense of sound, but deal
with it quite differently:

LISTENING

I lie listening--

    Cars sneak by in squeaky shoes,
        afraid to shatter the silent night.
    or thunder by, afraid of being
        swallowed by it.
    Under the house, a mother cat purrs
        to the feeding of her kittens.
    A train bellows a warning,
        its big, white eye forcing
        everyone to stop and watch
    And listen.

I lie listening--

    Cars crash,
    The white eye blinks.
    The mother cat screams of her
        children's murders,
    While a tom sits licking the
        flesh from his claws.

    Did Pelops have a mother?

45

I lie listening to her anguish.

--Claire Loe
10th Grade

SILENT SONG

That which you call the ritual of silence
is to me the sound of a thousand voices
that carry on the wind for miles,
so that I can catch them and listen.

And the song I hear is quiet,
But loudly so.
Forever is a song sung alone,
Or with you, another singer.

And in my silent song we sit,
held together by colored chords
that no one sees but me and you,
or maybe just me.

And the peaceful place in a crowded room
is my door opening on to the terrace,
filled with flowers
blooming like watercolors, all color, no sound.

And within my flower garden,
we share a table for two
and drink a cup of quiet song
for the music you call silence

--Jeauxdie Wilson
12th Grade

Exercise 6 - Synaesthesia Poems: We will begin this
exercise with some "warm-up" activites in the use of
synaesthesia. What (you ask with a look of horror on
your face) is synaesthesia? Relax--it is NOT a dread
disease; in fact, it is a very creative and enter-
taining form of sense-play. But, to answer your question, synaesthesia has been defined as "the description
of one kind of sensation in terms of another"; for
example, the description of sight in terms of touch,
as in a "cool green".

   Warm-Up Activity 1. Listen to voices, either
live or recorded. You might prefer to record your own
voice, and the voices of your friends, or listen to
recordings of vocalists. If you choose the latter
approach, be sure to select vocalists whose voices are
very different sounds, such as Janis Joplin, Joni
Mitchell, Kenny Loggins, Willie Nelson, Johnny Mathis.

46

Whichever approach you take, listen to the
voices very carefully, then make a list of reactions
to each voice in terms of taste, smell, touch, and
sight. Below are some samples of student reactions to
Kenny Loggin's voice:

What does his voice taste like?	What does his voice feel like?
hot fudge (note that this reaction includes touch) artichoke butterscotch butter	a puppy's belly spring rain on my face velvet rubbed against the nap

In reaction to Joni Mitchell's voice:

What does it look like?	What does it smell like?
yellow flowers beads of rain on a window- pane a rainbow	strawberries honeysuckle watermelon

O.K., now, you try it. If you compare your reactions
with those of your friends, you might note some similarities emerging: even if not, a synaesthesia is a
good exercise for sharpening your senses!

Writing Assignment: Now try to make a poem
out of a synaesthesia exercise of your own choice. You
might describe someone you know well through synaesthesia, as in the example below which describes a person
through the sense of taste:

VANILLA VAINLY

vanilla vainly pure practically clean dreams
chocolate delicious dark thoughts
strawberry passionate schemes
(rarely coffee mediocre)
chocolate chip contrast of love
and jealous pistachio bitter hate
butter pecan sex you are

you are cold hotfudgesauce
hardening on my teeth
dripping sticky down my now cup
messy stain on my tomorrow napkin

the cones from once soothing creams
prick the insides of my nostalgia stomach
which bleeds regret and yet
I eat the frozen hopes because you're gone
too quickly melt
my stomach, abused, overfilled and yet empty
ache, how sick I feel

47

by noon, another dip
of chocolate chip
another lick
of you
thirty cents a scoop
it adds up.

--Dana Smith
College Student

Perhaps you will want to use an object, such as in the
synaesthesia poem below, which describes the sound of a
musical instrument through the sense of color and sight.

SYNAESTHESIA HAIKU

The saxophone bulged
        A yellow noise, and spun
Green spirals sideways.

--Kevin Kuykendall
12th Grade

Perhaps you would prefer to describe a place or an
experience through synaesthesia, as these students did
in the poems below:

FOREST TONES

An intricacy of distant notes
    echoed in my ears
Colliding with sounds of blue and gray.
And they seemed a forest of dissonance,
                a cavern of endless echoes.

The forest, wrapped in web and dew, was
Coated with forgotten melodies
    beneath powdered rocks of green mold.
I existed in that world--deaf to its song,
And I ran from that forest
    searching for rainbow lollipops and clovers.
I left those mossy trees
    without ever hearing their chiming cries,
    without ever tasting the clovers beneath
        their roots.

Yet by happenstance, I heard your weed-drop song,
And I learned from your wooden guitar
    the melodies within your forest
        and within myself.
Together, we entered my forest of raw tones,
        my moss land of green and gray.
You showed me the berries, the lizards, and
        the weedflowers,

48

And we filled your guitar with clover,
And used some worn twine for strings.

Moist melodies soaked from your warm guitar,
    renewed my feeling of birth
And I rested on the clover
    and slept in my new sanctuary of youth.

The notes now ring clear and sweet
    between my vibrant leaves.
And I can swing from their harmonious limbs
And the songs that hear shall
    always hold me
    so tightly in my tiny
    forest of dreams.

                        --Carolyn Haynes
                          12th Grade

DAYBREAK: SYMPHONY

As the dreamy sway of the night-harp's enchantment
Fades to moody charcoal-gray,
Wary threads of violin coil tentatively in
    mid-air,
Spinning spidery flourishes around breathless
    silence.
--Silver slashes--
They are rent by the triumph of a single golden
    peal.
Warm bass defines the midnight depths,
And a fluted meadowlark pleads for the day.

                        --Julie Lee
                          10th Grade

Exercise 7 - A Photograph of the Senses: This is
an exercise that will help you put together your
skills observing and reacting through all of your
senses. The poem below was written in reaction to a
photograph of a very shy child who had very big, brown
eyes. Read the poem below very carefully.

SHY, LIKE A MARMOSET

Sometimes
you see these dark-eyed creatures
clinging to the smooth boles
of gum trees
with tiny hands as pink
as a baby's.
Sometimes,
when peering among broad leaves shining
in moonlight,

you may freeze one
in some quiet jungle ritual,
its round eyes like berries
bound to you with quivering threads,
its furry body curled
from elbow to toe.

You may want to touch it--
don't.
You may want to reach out
and hold it close to you
and carry it into the light
and study it
and nurture it--
don't.
They are wild and gentle creatures.
They thrive only in the stillness
of the darkwood deeps.

--Juliet Lee
11th Grade

Notice that the physical details of the photograph are
the basis of the sense details of the poem--taste,
touch, sound, smell, and sight.

Now you try it. Find a photograph, perhaps
one of your own, or one in a magazine or book, but be
sure you select one that really reaches you, speaks
to you. An excellent source for photographs are col-
lections such as The Family of Man or even human
interest photographs you might find in your local
newspaper.

Below are some poems written in response to
photographs:

INSPIRATION

A guitar leans against the wall, waiting:
The window is open.
The pattern of a shadow
Born of the light of a dying day
Dances across the bed.
On the desk, a candle glows
Applauding the wind
As it makes its entrance
Through the window.
The wind cautiously tiptoes from the flame,
Pauses before the guitar, contemplating,
Then slowly,
Delicately,

As gracefully as his own fingers,
It touches the strings--

If you bend your ear towards the very edge
    of sound
You can hear the guitar's tears, falling
    in the wind.

                        --David McLaughlin
                          11th Grade

SUNGLASSES

Lights glance off
Smooth, round glass,
and the sight of my
reflection
Makes me uneasy
Never softens with love
Or widens in fear
And never sparkles with laughter:
Cold silver,
Empty space,
And a sad excuse
For eyes.

                        --Karen King

Exercise 8 - Becoming Someone Else: Here is another
approach to using photographs as stimulus for writing
sense impressions. This time, instead of using surface details and observing as a spectator outside of
the photograph, try to enter right into the photograph,
into its mood and situation, even into the mind and
emotions of the person in the photograph. The story
below was a reaction to a photograph of a young man
sitting in a chair in an empty, deserted room:

THE GEPHYROPHOBIA SYNDROME

He listened carefully from where he was
perched on the edge of the uncomfortable
wicker chair. Somehow he knew that he
wouldn't hear anything, but he listened anyway. The voices were gone. He strained
his concentration to catch the lightest
hint of the wise old southern drawl, or the
nasally whine of the Jewish-mother voice.
He would've welcomed an argument from those
mismatched roommates (the ones that he had,
for so long, though lived above him--until
someone complained about his banging on the

ceiling with a broomstick in the middle of
the night). But they were gone. The voices,
his constant companions, those that soothed
and angered and bugged him, and were always
there--even though they weren't the best of
friends, at least he could count on them.
But not any more. They were gone.

The voices were gone, but that was not
the worst. Other things were no longer there.
His Oedipal complex, for example. He no
longer harbored a burning desire to see his
father buried, even to dig the grave, then
marry, make love to, and care for his mother.
He missed it, and it worried him.

He took his father's picture from its
hiding place in the coffee table drawer and
placed it on the mantel, hoping that it
would stir something he had managed to bury
deep within himself. Nothing. Not a
twinge of hatred, not even the slightest
sliver of jealousy. And his mother's picture, now only a mother and not a target
of his lust, wasn't beautiful, or even pretty.
He felt a loss.

The windows had become just windows, not
doors or walls or mirrors--just windows.
He could no longer look through the walls
and see the trash gather in the gutter. He
couldn't watch the hundreds of empty beer
cans pile up and threaten his house with
their sheer bulk. And he didn't care. He
no longer worried about being eaten by,
buried under, or simply run over by dirt
and trash. It was all very unusual.

Water no longer scared him. Nothing
frightened him anymore. Death didn't
frighten him. Neither did cats, or dogs,
for that matter, or men, women, heat, sun,
night, day, books, sex, rabies, sin, Dante,
or postage stamps. He wasn't even afraid
of being frightened. It confused him.

The little man that always hid in his
coat pocket had obviously moved out, because
he no longer felt the prickly sensation on
the back of his neck. The little man had
moved out and taken all of his little cameras.
He could tell no one was taking pictures anymore.

He wasn't angered or insulted, but he felt
a loss. Not only had the little man moved
out, but it didn't matter at all. He was
no longer afraid of being watched.

He shifted uncomfortably, trying to
figure out when and why all this had started
happening. Why was his world shifting, moving
and leaving him behind? When had it started
happening? He thought logically and clearly,
controlling his thoughts and easily separating
them from the sensory barrage around him.
There was no doubt that something unusual had
happened.

Fearing insanity, he started to panic.
The way he acted and thought surprised him.
Everything changed. Everything he knew,
counted on, or believed in became unnatural,
unreal. It was all so strange.

He contemplated suicide. That, too, was
strange. He had never thought about killing
himself before, though he had tried it twice.
And now, not only was he thinking about it,
but he was also talking himself out of it.

The teddy bear in his room had become
just a teddy bear. It no longer walked, or
talked, or peed on the floor like normal
teddy bears. It too had changed.

He didn't feel like playing with the
silver-ware, pretending to be a Doberman, or
dressing up in his mother's old costume
jewelry. He no longer saw visions of heaven
and hell. For the first time, he made a
beautiful dinner and did not just sit and
watch it get cold.

He knew this was a major point in his life,
an incident that he should not forget. His
life was turning around, even if he could not
tell whether it was a turn for the worse or
not.

"What's happening?" he asked aloud. His
voice was calm, but had an insistent edge to
it. He seemed to direct the question to the
easy chair in front of him. "What's happening
to me? Why is everything so unreal? So
unusual? What is it?"

He didn't really seem to be expecting an
answer, but when one didn't come, he was
hurt and shocked. Especially shocked. He
reached across to the balding easy chair
and slowly put his hand in the seat. The
cushion yielded to the pressure. He stood
up slowly and moved around the chair. Carefully he turned his back to it and, as
carefully as a yogi lowering himself onto a
bed of nails, he lowered himself into the
cushion. For a moment he sat mystified
and frightened, then he lowered his face
into his hands and his shoulders shook
with painful gulping sobs. This was definitely the worst.

What do you do, he wondered, when even
your imaginary playmate pretends you don't
exist.

--Eric Coleman
11th Grade

In the process of writing your piece on
"Becoming Someone Else," study the photograph you
select as your stimulus, and ask yourself questions
like this: Who is this person? Why is he doing
what he is doing? What is he like? What are his
thoughts? What is he feeling? Why is he feeling
what he is? Why is he thinking what he is? Are you
sensitive enough to become else, to put yourself
in someone else's soul? Try it, and see what
happens.

Below are some student examples; the first
poem used as stimulus a photograph of bears in a
cage at the zoo:

THE PLACE WHERE TIME MOVES SLOWEST

The animals hear each falling sand
in the hourglass.
watch each moment that a falling sand marks.

The gorilla shut her ears
pushing her black fingers
deep into the sides of her face.
She shut her eyes
pressing her eyelids together tighter than
any clenched fist
Her dry nose exploded breath
and her tight jaw looked ready to crush inward

but the crowds just cooed.
"Sweet man-beast, sweet girl."

    The lioness stretched long and lean
    over her rock pedestal
    She was the first dying goddess
    I've ever seen.
    Her amber eyes focused
    on an unmarked piece of sky.
    Maybe she looked for the heaven
    of Serrenghetti plains and long-legged
      gazelles.
    But the crows just threw
    peanut shells in her face.

The animals count to infinity
sand
by
sand, while the civilized beasts . . .
the people . . . eat cotton candy and laugh.

                --Christine Kim
                  11th Grade

This poem was written in reaction to a rocking chair
on an empty beach:

                PAPA

Rocking chair kills
          slowly.
You didn't know.
    Television
        and
         Reader's Digest
Didn't tell you . . .
              anything.
Maybe now
    There's a life
             After
                So
                  Much
                    Death.

            --Elizabeth Plaag

    A photograph of a nude suggested the poem
below:

             SCREAMING

It wakes me in the black hours
before dawning--
like a wailing siren, ambulance keening;

her silent screaming
rips the gauze net of sleep,
tears Dream, my lover, from my arms.
Electricity out, a candle's all I have
to look for her.
I find her
huddled in a corner,
face paler than her pale nightdress,
wide eyes red-rimmed,
mouth shut tight.
Her fingers raking claw-like
through a wild tangle
of hair, she rocks, moans,
a child lost and alone in the dark.
I come a little closer,
holding the candle before me
like a cross.
It echoes in the stillness
in my head
her silent screaming
I see it in her eyes, ringing
rising and falling
she's drowning in the darkness
and she opens her mouth
but no sound comes out
and I come a little closer
till my sudden breathing fogs over
the mirror, puts out
the flame
and I'm alone
in the dark with
my silent screaming.

--Juliet Lee
12th Grade

All right. Do you get the idea of how important it
is to translate the world of concepts, that is,
thoughts, ideas, feeling, into the world of senses?
With the practice you've done in this chapter in using
senses to express concepts, you should be ready to try
more complicated uses of the senses in the next
chapter.

FOOTNOTES - CHAPTER III

[1]Robert Shutes and Bernard R. Tanner,
Critical Thinking (Menlo Park, CA: Addison-Wesley
Publishing Co., 1973), 3.

[2] May Swenson, "Early Morning: Cape Cod,"
To Mix With Time (New York: Charles Scribner's Sons,
1963), 132-33.

[3]Carl Sandburg, "Under the Harvest Moon,"
Complete Poems (New York: Harcourt, Brace and World,
Inc., 1950), 49.

[4]Oscar Wilde, "Symphony in Yellow," The
Portable Oscar Wilde, Richard Aldington, ed. (New
York: The Viking Press, 1946), 586.

CHAPTER IV

IMAGINATION:
LATERAL THINKING TECHNIQUES

Lateral thinking is closely associated to the right brain functions of imagination, creativity, and spontaneous Gestalts of sudden flashes of insight. Edward de Bono observes that lateral thinking "is as definite a way of using the mind as logical thinking", or as the left brain function of vertical, sequential logic.[1]

Below is an excerpt from de Bono's book, Lateral Thinking, which gives an excellent summary of the differences between lateral (right brain) and vertical (left brain) thinking:

Differences between lateral and vertical thinking

Since most people believe that traditional vertical thinking is the only possible form of effective thinking it is useful to indicate the nature of lateral thinking by showing how it differs from vertical thinking. Some of the most outstanding points of difference may seem sacrilegious:

1. Vertical thinking is selective; lateral thinking is generative.

   Rightness is what matters in vertical thinking; Richness is what matters in lateral thinking. . . .

2. Vertical thinking moves only if there is a direction in which to move; lateral thinking moves in order to generate a direction.

   With vertical thinking one moves in a clearly defined direction towards the solution of a problem. One uses some definite approach or some definite technique. With lateral thinking one moves for the sake of moving. One does not have to be moving towards something, one may be moving away from something. It is the movement or change that matters. . . .

59

3. Vertical thinking is analytical; lateral thinking is provocative.

4. Vertical thinking is sequential; lateral thinking can make jumps.

5. With vertical thinking one has to be correct at every step; with lateral thinking one does not have to be.

6. With vertical thinking one uses the negative in order to block off certain pathways; with lateral thinking there is no negative.

7. With vertical thinking one concentrates and excludes what is irrelevant; with lateral thinking one welcomes chance intrusions.

8. With vertical thinking categories, classification and labels are fixed; with lateral thinking they are not.

   Vertical thinking depends heavily on the rigidity of definitions just as mathematics does on the unalterable meaning of a symbol once this has been allocated. Just as a sudden change of meaning is the basis of humour so an equal fluidity of meaning is useful for the stimulation of lateral thinking.

9. Vertical thinking follows the most likely paths; lateral thinking explores the least likely.

10. Vertical thinking is a finite process; lateral thinking is a probabilistic one.

Summary:

   The differences between lateral and vertical thinking are very fundamental. The processes are quite distinct. It is not a matter of one process being more effective than the other for both are necessary. It is a matter of realizing the differences in order to be able to use both effectively.

60

Lateral thinking is not a substitute
for vertical thinking. Both are required.
They are complementary.

Lateral thinking enhances the effective-
ness of vertical thinking. Vertical thinking
develops the ideas generated by lateral
thinking. You cannot dig a hole in a different
place by digging the same hole deeper. Vertical thinking is used to dig the same hole
deeper. Lateral thinking is used to dig a
hole in a different place.[2]

Obviously, then, lateral thinking is directly
concerned with the generation of new ideas, with
breaking out of the "concept prisons of old ideas,"
with "looking in a different way at things which have
always been looked at in the same way."[4] De Bono
observes that freedom from old ideas and the generation of new ideas are dual gestures of lateral
thinking.

The purpose of this chapter is to show that
lateral thinking is a very basic part of "whole brain"
knowing, and that by practicing lateral thinking
techniques, one can develop skill in it. Instead of
simply wishing for imagination, creativity and
insight, you can develop and call upon those right
brain functions through the use of lateral thinking.

Imagination and Creativity

To know is nothing at all;
    To imagine is everything.

                    --Anatole France

Sensing--observing--responding--all are
crucial to good writing, as well as being essential
to aware, centered living. But let's face it,
bothering to notice and bothering to respond is not
enough; even animals sense and respond to the senses.
It is not enough to simply see objects, or to perceive
the facts of our physical experience; it is not even
enough to be able to form the concepts, to find the
words, to re-create that sense or that perception for
others. If you stop there, you get trapped in the
outer world, the left brain world, and you cheat
yourself of that rich, many-hued, wondrous world

61

within--the world of right brain function: the world of dream, fantasy, intuition, insight, the world of imagination.

What Is Imagination?

Imagination is a word that is thrown around a lot, but what does it mean--really? Simply stated, imagination is the power to see things in new, fresh, or original relationships; that is, the power to associate percepts and concepts in new ways.

For centuries, writers, literary critics, and psychologists have debated the nature of imagination, especially such issues as: what is the relationship between imagination and reason or the intellect? How is it different from fantasy, or as the Romantics called it, fancy? Does imagination transcend the reality of the sense? These are fascinating and complex questions and give testimony to the fact that even today imagination involves human powers no one fully understands. In this chapter, we'll experiment with some of these issues so that you may arrive at some answers for yourself concerning the nature of imagination.

Granting the mysterious and unknown qualities of imagination, there seems to be agreement that imagination is "a blinding and unifying . . . power of the mind which enables [us] to see inner relationships . . . a shaping and ordering power, the function of which is to give art its special authority. . . . The assumption is almost always present that the 'new' creation shaped by the imagination is a new form of reality, not a fantasy or a fanciful project."[3]

Who is more qualified to tell us about imagination than good old Willie Shakespeare? In the passage below from A Midsummer's Night Dream, he gives two samples of "strong imagination":

> The lunatic, the lover, and the poet
> Are of imagination all compact.
> One sees more devils than vast Hell can hold,
> That is the madman. The lover, all as
>   frantic,
> See Helen's beauty in a brow of Egypt.
> The poet's eye, in a fine frenzy rolling,

Doth glance from Heaven to Earth, from
    Earth to Heaven,
And as imagination bodies forth
The forms of things unknown, the poet's pen
Turns them to shapes, and gives to airy nothing
A local habitation and a name.
Such tricks hath strong imagination
That if it would be apprehend some joy,
It comprehends some bringer of that joy;
Or in the night, imagining some fear,
How easy is a bush supposed a bear.[4]

There is much said about imagination in
the passage that is worth discussing.[5] First,
let's look at the two examples Shakespeare gives
of "strong imagination." Can you identify with
the first example? You know, he's the one who
anticipates (apprehends) some joy so keenly that
he reads/comprehends the answer in the face and
manner of the one who brings the joy, such as a
child or lover can see in the face of another the
fulfillment of his dreams and hopes. The other example is the person who is consumed by an imaginary
fear at night that changes a familiar object into
a frightening one. Doubtless you've had your turns
with both kinds of these experiences of "strong
imagination." In fact, much literature and many
popular songs, films, and television shows seem
to be recreations of these experiences. Can you
name some? First, let's try T.V. and films. To
get you started, how about "Tommy", that classic
film by the Who, and look at The Star Wars' series,
the horror films . . . and popular songs? How
about "War of the Worlds" or Kenny Loggins'
"Nightwatch"? Examples in literature abound: Edgar
Allan Poe's "The Raven", and all of his horror
tales; Samuel Taylor Coleridge's "Kubla Khan",
Washington Irving's "The Headless Horseman", to name
only a few.

Exercise 1: In your journal, write an account of
each of the following:

A) Present, with as much detail as you can,
   an experience you had with a "night fear",
   a time when familiar sights and sounds
   transformed themselves into a moment of
   uncertainty or terror.

B) Present, in detail, an experience in which you anticipated joy so strongly that your imagination tricked you into seeing what you wanted to see, whether it was there or not.

C) Select a person--real, historic, or imaginary--and imagine that that person were here with you right now. What would you say to him/her and he/she to you? Write an imaginary conversation that sounds real.

These exercises demonstrate that we all have strong imagination, and there is nothing wrong with that. Still, having an imagination doesn't make you a lover--or a poet--or (thank goodness!) a lunatic! Madmen--lovers--poets use their imaginations in individual ways: indeed they are, in various degrees and ways, dominated and controlled by their imaginations.

We are concerned with the imagination of the writer. Let's go back to Shakespeare's quote for a moment. What did he say about the imagination of a poet? How does the poet differ from the rest of mankind? Shakespeare says:

And as imagination bodies forth
The forms of things unknown, the poet's pen
Turns them to shapes, and gives to airy nothing
A local habitation and a name.

Shakespeare says the writer gives form to the experiences that imagination brings him. He not only invents the "unreal" and the unique by recombining the elements of this "real" world, he gives "to airy nothing a local habitation"--a place in our physical, real worlds and "a name", an identity, a reality.

In short, the writer doesn't just imagine, he writes. Writing is the form we give our imagination. It is in the process of writing, of bringing the outer world of sense into balance with the inner world of imagination, insight, perception and intuition, that centering unfolds. The clay doesn't center itself; it is a "doing" process. So is writing. So is living a centered life. The following exercises, hopefully, should get you started on transforming imagination into words, of finding appropriate, effective ways of sharing your vision and your insight.

Imagination Warm-Up Exercises: These activities will get your imagination "warmed-up" for the heavier stuff to follow. You may do these warm-ups in a group or independently, but you should record your responses/reactions/outcomes in your journal. Remember: imagination is the key.

Warm-up #1 - How many uses can you think of for . . .

a brick?
or an empty can?
or a garden hose?
or (fill in your choice)?

Warm-Up #2 - Can you devise a way to open a garage door automatically, using all of the following elements?

lawn sprinkler
front end of automobile
garage door (sliding variety)
hose and water outlet
dog sleeping on table
mallet
pistol and bullet
goldfish aquarium
exploding cap
rabbit with nearby burrow
string and rope
can full of water
cork
see-saw
at least one flea

(Are you getting warmed-up?)

Warm-Up #3 - Choose one of the situations below: Imagine that you are waiting for a bus on the street in front of a large department store. A stranger approaches you and asks, "Why have you been following me?" You try to ignore him, then you attempt to deny his accusations, but he becomes more and more insistent. Finish the fantasy by writing a short short story based on this situation, including the dialogue between you and the stranger.

65

Curiosity prompts you and a friend to enter a
deserted house. You are prowling through its rooms
when you come across a box with a rusty old lock.
You pull on the lock, and it falls off. As your
blood begins to tingle, you pry up the creaking
lid. What do you find? What happens then? Finish
the fantasy by writing a short short story based
on the situation, including a description and dialogue between you and your friend.

(Getting warmer?)

Warm-Up #4 - Fantasize a conversation
between . . . your journals and your pen, then choose
one of the following and do the same:

1.   a bulldozer and an old building about to
     be torn down
2.   a can of stewed tomatoes and a rib-eye
     steak at the grocery store
3.   a caterpillar and a stone

Whew . . . I think you must be warm enough! Now
let's think a minute. Instead of just imagining,
look at each warm-up activity, think about your
process of doing it, and respond to these questions:

1.   Which warm-up was "the easiest?" Why do
     you think it was least difficult?
2.   Which warm-up was "the most fun"? Why do
     you think it was?
3.   Which warm-up required the most logic,
     reason, "thought"? Why?
4.   Which warm-up seemed to require the most
     imagination, creativity and originality?
     Why do you say that?
5.   Which warm-up do you feel was "most suc-
     cessful" in warming your imagination up?
     Why?

Can you reach any conclusions or generalizations?
Have you learned anything about yourself through
these warm-up activities and through thinking about
them? If so, what?

Brain as Programmer

Any discussion of the thinking process,
whether it be lateral (right brain) or logical (left
brain) thinking, would not be complete without con-
sidering how the brain prepares to receive new ideas,

or to generate new ways of seeing old information.

Recent brain research on hemispheric differentiation shows that the left brain, like a computer, creates, organizes and assimilates new information into existing patterns and frameworks. Once these patterns are formed and used, they become more and more firmly established. In short, the brain becomes a "programmer". Galyean explains it this way:

> The brain seems to operate on a programmatic basis. The information stored within the cell soma of each neuron represents not only isolated bits of information, but chains of information as well. When we perform a simple activity like batting an eyelash, millions of circuits are triggered simultaneously--just the precise ones we need to perform the desired activity. As we practice new skills, acquiring new information, entire chains of stored material called programs become available for continual use. [6]

How the brain selects its programs is fascinating and is what has tremendous implications to us in centering and in the development of whole brain knowing and thinking. Brain researchers tell us that the brain operates, selects its programs, on a emotional bias system:

> Only that information that is perceived by the learner as helpful, interesting, and rewarding and/or gamey is eventually processed by the brain. In short, we learn what we want to learn. [7]

Obviously, then, our willingness to hold our mind open to new information, to new ideas, to experiment with new patterns of thinking is crucial to getting the maximum use of our brain. How is this accomplished? Again, brain research gives us some clues in the use of open focusing techniques.

Open Focusing Techniques

Research indicates that the brain does not require our conscious, left-brain effort to allow right brain information to be encoded in the brain; it requires only our attention, our openness to let the information through, and then process it in the left brain verbally so it can be remembered, or programmed. A good example of this open focus concept is the common phenomena of the attempt to remember our dreams. Dreaming is a specialized function of the right brain. Dreams are non-verbal and are expressed entirely in images and symbols. We've all had the experience of waking from a dream, vividly recalling the dream, falling back asleep, and being unable to recall the dream the next morning upon waking.

Blakeslee's research on dreaming and hemispheric differentiation verified his premise that "verbally recalling dreams that originate in the right brain requires a transferral of images from the right brain into words in the left brain."[8] Hence, most people who say that they don't dream are not maintaining an "open focus"; they are not programming their left brain to transfer the right-brain images to their verbal consciousness.

An interesting experiment at the University of Edinburgh reinforces the open focus concept. Before testing, the subjects were classified as to thinking style: one group was scientifically oriented, logical, primarily left-brain thinkers, while the other group was classified as lateral, more creative, primarily right brain thinkers. Each time their eye movements indicated they were dreaming, the subjects were awakened and asked to describe their dreams. The left brain types could only describe their dreams 65% of the time, while the right brain types recalled 95.2% of their dreams.[9]

Again and again, research verifies that through open focusing, dreams can be remembered, and much of the right brain's nonverbal knowledge and activity can be retrieved and used by keeping our attention open and focused on it.

Below are some exercises to help you focus on the knowledge and rich world of information offered you in your dreams, and a process to help you retrieve and use that information:

Exercise 1 - Dream Journal: Keep your journal or a
tape-recorder by your bed. Each time you awaken
from a dream, describe in as much detail as possible
the dream, either on tape on in your journal. The
verbal process of description will allow the information to be encoded in the left brain. Be sure to
date each dream.

Exercise 2 - Dream Workshop: This exercise might
be an unfamiliar experience to you. People tend
to conceal their fantasies (sleeping and waking
dreams) from each other and to keep their imaginations secret. But to become centered, you need to
develop this sense of sharing your vision and your
dreams; in short, you need to practice some self-
awareness, at least as much as you comfortably
can.

The purpose of this exercise is to share
fragments of your dreams and produce written material
based on them. Here is a suggested process:

Step 1: Set up an environment that is
informal and comfortable for a dream sharing session
with a small group of people. Turn the lights low
or off, sit in a circle on the floor in groups of
5-7 per group.

Step 2: Each person in the group recalls
at least one dream, daydream and/or fantasy and
communicates it to the group. No effort is made to
analyze or interpret these dreams; simply experience them and share them with one another.

Step 3: Now try to develop a story or a
poem based on a dream or fantasy you have had.
Below is a student poem that grew out of such a
dream:

A DREAM MEETING WITH THE WINTER GIRL SOLDIER

And sleep took me to future
from present past walled limits
of my room. Here, there is only
the northern cold that lies
upon naked skin like
a veil of ice. The hazy
grey of morning makes the
snow shadows black and blue.

And I cannot move inside
This field of blue ice. My muscles

vibrate as wind slides over
skin and flesh, both of the soft,
shielding stuff of fighting soldiers.

On a road that ends into this field,
a dark form walks over hard, packed snow.
The small child's woollen army coat,
too large to hold a single life,
drags behind her on the ground.
The visor of the officer's hat
rests over her eyes as if to mask
sight from sightlessness.

She touches the narrow road as would
a dying breath escaped from a blinded
soldier's mouth. She cracks the
air with speech made of the brittle
rip of machineguns: "Are you
a woman? Have you pledged yourself to be?"
"No," I say.
"Then, prove to me you are a woman."
Snowflakes clung like dying butterflies
to her faded green. "Prove to me
we can be at peace."
"There is no war."
The child soldier points to summer grass
frozen straight like polished bayonets
stabbing at the sky. "Prove to me
we are inseparable soldiers."
For, here, there is only northern cold
that lies upon naked skin like a veil
of ice. And sleep releases me
into present walled limits to my room.

                              --Beth Barber
                              12th Grade

Here is another student example:

FIGURES IN THE NIGHT

Hideous laughing faces,
    mouths contorted in eternally pained smiles,
Discuss their sins and giggle.
A nudge in the ribs, the wind of an eye,
    and the offer of their hated, selfish
                        attempts at love,
And they laugh harder at the joke.

(I huddle tightly under my covers)

The crying faces,
Blood red tears saturating the bed's sheets,
  staining my naked body with their wrongs.
They ask nothing, offer no clues to what I face.
They serve only to scare me,
                    ruin my only sheets.

(I wash my bedding daily)

And the insane faces,
  laughing and crying,
ripping tears and giggles out of me
  as they would gut a fish.
Dancing heavily heavily over my chest and face,
  seducing me with their many colors
So that their flashing teeth might draw blood
  while I offer no resistance--
                    even help.

(I rip the sheets to bind my wounds)

But they are night figures,
And flee at the break of day,
So that I might make my bed and
                    await the fall of night.

                    --Eric Coleman
                      10th Grade

Alpha Production

     The point has been made earlier in this
chapter that the brain functions on a programmatic
basis. Besides the open focus concept, how may the
brain be conditioned or prepared to receive new
input, new ideas, new material? According to
Beverly Galyean:

     In order for change to take place within
     any system there must be sufficient flexibi-
     lity to allow old behavioral patterns to
     mollify, eventually break down, and give way
     to the appearance or creation of new forms.
     Through dissipation--breakdown and creation--
     neural patterns are reshaped; new neural
     circuits are created; thinking changes and
     progresses. The brain performs dissipative
     action through the creation of electronic
     waves. When we are in the ordinary waking
     state of conscious analytical thinking, short,
     rapid and rather rhythmic beta waves are pro-
     duced, allowing little or no room for

71

perturbation of the already existing patterns;
however, when we are deeply relaxed, engaged
in reverie or musing, fantasy or creative
endeavors, intuitive thinking or symbolic
expression our brain emits long, rapid waves
called alpha waves. These waves shake up
already existing patterns allowing new ones
to emerge. The alpha state is the sine qua
non exponent of creativity, insight and
illumination. Many of the greatest minds
of our time such as Aristotle, Galileo,
Copernicus, Newton and Einstein all priori-
tized the importance of reverie, fantasy,
imagination and intuition as the foundation
for new knowledge. Studies of highly intelligent people have shown that these people
tend to produce more alpha waves and work in
an alpha state for longer periods of time
than do persons of average intelligence.

It is possible that by providing students
with activities for inducing alpha consciousness, by allowing mood music, soft lighting,
and mental colors such as yellow, blue and
violet to adorn the room, and to encourage
deep breathing, centering, inner focusing
and imaging, we may be able to influence
both the rapidity and quantity of information being retained over long periods of
time.[10]

Following are activities which will induce
alpha production, stimulation of the right brain
functions of creativity, imagination and insight,
then bridge these functions with the left brain
through writing.

Exercise 1 - Go With the Music: Have you ever
noticed how much music affects your mood, or how it
can take you to another world? Music is an excellent stimulus for imagining, daydreaming, and
fantasizing. This exercise gives you permission
to do just that--all you want! Here is a suggested
process:

Step 1: Select instrumental music which
gives you a wide range of moods. Song lyrics tend
to limit and influence your imagination, so go
with instrumental only. Below are some suggested
musical selections that have worked well:

Carlos Santana:
  "Europa" from <u>Moonflower</u>
  "Aquamarine" from <u>Marathon</u>
  "Future Primitive" from <u>Caravanserai</u>

Jean Michel Jarre:
  <u>Equinoxe</u>, Part I
  <u>Oxgene</u>, Part I

Hogaku Yonin No Kai:
  "Kiso-Bussti", <u>Koto Melodies of Japan</u>

Steve Halpern:
  <u>Spectrum Suite</u>
  <u>Starborn Suite</u>

Mason Williams:
  "Sunflower", <u>The Mason Williams Phonograph
  Record</u> and "Classical Gas"

Jr. Walker and the All Stars:
  "Cleo's Mood", <u>Shotgun</u>

The Mystic Moods Orchestra:
  "Far from the Madding Crowd", "Clare de Lune",
  "Love Theme from the Sand Pebbles", Wednes-
  day's Child", "Theme from A Man and A
  Woman", from <u>More than Music</u>
  "Tristan and Isolde" from the <u>Mystic Moods of
  Love</u>

Pink Floyd:
  "Echoes" from <u>Meddle</u>

Paul Weston:
  "Storyville" from <u>Crescent City</u>

Paul Horn
  "Inside"

The Alan Parsons Project:
  "A Dream within a Dream", "The Fall of the
  House of Usher", <u>Tales of Mystery and
  Imagination - Edgar Allan Poe</u>
  "Voyager", "Pyramania" and "Hyper-Gamma-
  Spaces" from <u>Pyramid</u>

Vivaldi:
  "Four Seasons" by Jesse Stearne

  <u>Step 2</u>: After selecting 5-10 musical pieces
which offer a variety of mood; play each piece at least
twice. As you listen, let the music take you away with
it. Are you alone in a particular setting? a situation?
Are you alone or with someone? Create the scene in your
mind as vividly as possible, using your five senses to
make it "real".

Step 3: After your "scene" or fantasy is very real to you, as the music is still playing, jot down your sense impressions. What can you see, hear, smell, touch, taste in the scene? Don't worry about grammar or constructions or spelling; don't even worry about writing sentences. Just get the senses down.

Step 4: Now from the 5-10 reactions you had, select one sense impression that is strongest or most interesting to you. Develop it into either a short narrative or a poem. To do this, you are confronted with the major concern of every writer who is dealing with imaginary content: How does a writer make the world of imagination as real as the "real" world of our senses? The answer is simple: Appeal to the senses of your reader so that he may see, hear, taste, smell, and feel that imaginative world as vividly as you do. Translate the world of imagination into a world of the senses. Center.

Below is a student poem. As you read it, can you hear Vivaldi's "Autumn" in the background?

AUTUMN MORNING OVER LAKE STYX

I

Night hung
heavy and
cold. The
lake clear
            and still as a mirror
And every breath solid down like
                vertical razors
Nothing stirred or
offered a
comforting
whisper.
                On the shore, my only
form crouched on the wet grass--
                huddling over
                huddling over
                gray ash
Staring at a stubborn red ember.

II

I heard the sudden call
of the wild duck that came
as night lost to the blue morning fog

74

Its echo touched
         the hills
              and northing maples
and drifted through my old eyes

              The call
so simple
and complete
                   so distant

as to shut all
perception out.

III

A second call
came over me hard
like a million life-times.

              And every nerve
              end pulsed with
              silent need

The silk duck lifted her brown wings--
The sky caught and pulled
a free life into gray fields.

         She faded
a form
                   a dot
         a speck
                        and nothing at all.
A complete and simple passage.

IV

Dawn.
The sun edged
over illusionary
ends. Red and gold
leaves seemed
         to vibrate with light
And every breath slid down
                   cool

The lake changed its facade to light blue

              And I remained
              gazing past a
              red fire

hearing in a clear, gray sky, the call
                   of a wild duck.

                        --Beth Barber
                        12th Grade

75

Note how the writer made the senses real; she has put us there, made us observe the sense and respond to it, so it is no longer imaginary. Now you try it.

This piece was suggested by "Atmospheres" in 2001: A Space Odyssey:

LIFEBURN

It was always coffee-black between the two sections of hallway. Whirling, colors formed in my eyes and spun as my pupils tried to adjust to light that wasn't there.

Ahh . . . .

Light. Not much, truly, but no longer must I merely feel my way down the corridors. My footsteps were the best of a hollow heartdrum as they echoed in the square yellow tube. The walls were rough in the places where the cement had oozed between the plywood planks used in construction. Leaking perpetually through a thin place in the ceiling, an alkaloid, sharply-scented drip of water pierced the death silence with a plop, plop.

My ship waited in this hell beneath the earth. Sargent-Master had built a fine half-ton combination lock a century ago, but the one on the hanger door jammed with every turn of its two-foot tumbler wheel. My shirt clung wetly to my back and shoulders by the time the monolith-door sank away into the floor.

The ship. Dirty where oil leaked through loose couplings. My ship. But the engines gleamed and chimed when I tapped one, and the next.

Departure. Clank, lock, zip, snap, strap, ready?

The hanger ceiling slid back to let in the low-lying city fog. And I flew. The walls, fog, ground, buildingcitystate . . . world spiraled away beneath me. Space is neither cool nor hot. It simply is. Hot is the word I'll use for the sun. The sun hot, my ship was a streak of molten metal, still hundreds of kilometers away.

I was not gone, for . . .

I watch myself do this again, again, again,
again, again. . . .

--Gavin Doughtie
11th Grade

Exercise 2 - Fantasy Cards: This exercise is similar
to the one you just completed, except instead of
using music to stimulate your imagination, we'll use
a visual image called "Fantasy Cards." Perhaps you
have had a set of these cards; they may be pur-
chased through Pomegranite Press, or at any well-
stocked card shop. Or, you may wish to find your
own fantasy card, one that speaks strongly to you
in either a negative or positive way. You may
be strongly attracted to or even violently repulsed
by the card. The major criteria for selection of
your card is a strong response on an emotional level.

After you have made your selection, simply
let the card work on your imagination. Where does
the card take you? What does it suggest to you?
What do you feel? What effects do colors, forms,
images have on you? What do you think is going on?
Enjoy your fantasy, then try to reconstruct it in
words, either narratively or poetically. But remember what you just learned in Exercise 3: for your
fantasy to be real to someone else, you must use
appeal to the senses.

Exercise 3 - A Guided Fantasy: This exercise will
be a warm-up to the one which follows. Just relax,
free your mind as much as possible, and simply
follow the instructions below. You will need someone to read these instructions to you, and they
should be read slowly so that you do not feel rushed.
Also, the lights should be turned low and the exercise should be done in silence.

Here are the instructions: "Mill around the
room without contacting anyone. Imagine that you
are wading in water. Splash around a bit. Get the
feel of the water. Now the water is rising to cover
your feet. Do you feel it? It's up to your knees
now. Feel the difference in the way you walk and
move. The water has risen to your thighs now and
is at your groin. Feel the water with your finger-
tips. It continues to slowly rise and is at your
chest; now only your head is above water. Feel the

spaces around your head; keep moving. Now the
water completely covers your head but you are still
able to breathe. The water is beginning to recede
now, your head is completely out of the water.
Feel your space; you're dripping. Now the water is
at your waist; now at your groin; now at your thighs;
now at your knees; now at your ankles; now you are
standing in a puddle again. Relax and come back to
the present."11

Now, how did you react to that guided
fantasy?

Write down where you were, what you felt,
who you were with, what sensations you had. Was it
pleasant or unpleasant? Were you comfortable or
frightened? Why? The point of this warm-up is to
illustrate how our imaginations work in very unique,
original and independent ways. It is this somewhat
mysterious aspect of imagination that gives each
writer his own creative, original, unique vision.
Don't be afraid of it--it is a writer's gift, the
person's unique self.

Exercise 4 - Group Fantasy: The purpose of this
exercise is to give you practice in self-disclosure,
so you will need a group to do this exercise. Self-
disclosure is most clearly done when you tell others
directly how you are reacting to the present situation. Yet many times we reveal ourselves in indirect
ways, for example, by the jokes we tell, the things
we find funny, the television shows we watch, the
fantasies we have. The following exercise lets you
use your imagination in ways that may lead you to
a greater awareness of yourselves and which may help
you get to know one another in a different and interesting way. Below is a suggested procedure:

Step 1: Organize a group of 5-7 people.

Step 2: Someone volunteers to present an
unfinished situation, or even the beginning sentence
of a fantasy.

Step 3: Each person in the group adds to
the fantasy, and must take up the fantasy where the
person before him leaves off. It is important not
to get competitive in the fantasy exercise; simply
let your imagination take the fantasy in whatever
direction it goes. The last person in the group to
respond is responsible for finishing or ending the
fantasy.

Step 4: Repeat this process until everyone in the group has presented the beginning of a fantasy and everyone has ended a fantasy. The simplest way of doing this is to simply go around the circle by turns.

Step 5: In the group as a whole, discuss what you learned about yourself and other group members with regard to imagination and fantasy.

1. I am walking down a dark street. Up ahead I see a streetlight; the only sounds are my footsteps against the pavement and the distant hum of the city.

2. As I entered the party, I was overwhelmed by the noise--dance music, talking, laughter, ice cubes chattering in glasses . . . and by the stuffy heat. I took off my coat and scanned the room.

3. I didn't want to go to the rock concert in the first place, but . . .

4. Here I am once again, sitting in this boring dull Math class! If something doesn't happen soon, I'll die of boredom!

5. O.K.--you don't like those? Then try your own--yours are better anyway, and that is the point!

Be Self-Indulgent--and Freely Fantasize

Usually we are forced to function in the world of reality, but let's be self-indulgent in the last exercises in this chapter.

Exercise 1 - Play God--Create Your Own Fairy Tale:
It has been observed that fairy tales are the purest and simplest expression of the creative imagination of an individual. Support of this theory exists in the fact that fairy tales are universal; they exist in abundance in every language, in every culture, from every age; and generally all fairy tales contain certain basic elements which you need to keep in mind:

1. A beginning which states time and place, such as "once upon a time. . . ." That phrase really means a point of timelessness and spacelessness--the nowhere of the imagination.

79

Sometimes the beginning is expressed more specifically and poetically, such as:

> "At the end of the world, where the world comes to an end with a wall of boards. . . ."

or

> "In a time when God still walked about the earth. . . ."

But generally all fairy tales are marked by this sense of nowhereness, that timeless eternity, now and ever.

2. The people involved--look closely at how many main characters are involved, what their relationships are, who are the "good" people and who are the "bad" ones.

3. The conflict or plot--this includes the ups and downs of the story--the events--what happens?

4. The ending--interestingly enough, not all fairy tales end happily, as one would expect a fairy tale to do.

Can you remember your favorite fairy tale as a child? Consider the following points:

1. Which character do you identify with most in your favorite tale? Why do you identify with that character?

2. What do you like most about the particular fairy tale?

3. What similarities do you see in the tales presented?

4. What differences?

5. Can you compare them to the four elements of fairy tales discussed earlier?

6. Can you reach any conclusions?

O.K., now for the fun part: play God and create your imaginary kingdom, your own characters and a conflict for them to experience. Enjoy!

Below are some fairy tales written by students:

OF LEPRECHAUNS AND OTHER THINGS

. . . Where unicorns chase rainbows
And don't care about the pot of gold,

> by Ian Stallworth, published post-
> humously in A Tribute to Radiologist
> Apprentice Stallworth: We See The
> Beauty. Reprinted with permission
> from Unicorn Press.

#

Ian Stallworth quickly scribbled a note on a small pad of paper.

> Fredrika dearest,
> They've found the scout, but I've gotten away. I doubt you'll ever get this, but you can never be too sure. I've seen a rainbow--I think, and I know there are some unicorns out there somewhere. If I find them, I'll be back--probably. Got to get going--wish you had come.
>
> Love you,
>
> Ian.

He tore the note out and placed it on the driver's panel of the three story vehicles he had stolen. He picked up Freddy II's cage, draped a radiation cloak over it, zipped up his own rad-suit, checked the exposure level of his film (it was still under red-line radiation poison was at a minimum), and got out of the scout. He trotted, with his bulky equipment and mouse's cage, over the crest of the closest hill, just in time to see two more scouts and twenty-five rad-suited people on foot come over the horizon and spot the stolen scout. Feeling that it was useless to stay and watch them ransack the scout, he decided to move on.

Ian studied the wasteland and opted for a second opinion. "Which way," he asked. He gazed into Freddy II's cage and was met by a pair of uncomprehending beady eyes.

"Never mind," Ian said, "I'll decide myself."

He tossed a coin, and, seeming satisfied with the result, aimed himself toward a clump of far-off rocks, and started walking to the incessant chatter of his built-in geiger counter.

"A big help you are," Ian said.

"Squeak?"

#

A universe of twenty miles by twenty miles, deep underground, and only 150,000 people. He couldn't handle it. He knew it had been different, before the war. Before the germs and radiation and gasses covered the globe like one big cloud. He knew that an entire planet had been open, and lived on. And that even more had existed, and that people had reached up, off the planet, to enlarge their space. He knew how it had been, and he couldn't handle it now.

He read a lot, about before the war. About the wonders of nature, and all that had existed before. About leprechauns, fast food, centaurs, faeries, rainbows, and unicorns. He was fascinated by nature and natural things. He came to detest the cold, steel walls that enclosed him, even if his life did depend on them. So engrossed with nature had he become, that he wanted to tell others about it and open their lives to the wonders that nature wrought. But it was not to be done.

The lifeless steel now protected everyone. Nature was now hostile and inhospitable. No matter how technology once killed, it was not important, and any writing that was going to sell had to be based on the technological aspects of their lives.

He wanted so desperately to write, but he couldn't do _that_.

As he trudged through the desolate land, conversations reconstructed themselves in his mind.

#

"Listen here, Radiologist Nam was generous to offer you the apprenticeship. It's what you need to get your mind off that anti-tech junk . . ."

82

"Come on, Dad! I don't want to get off
that anti-tech junk! And I don't want to . . ."

"I don't care! You'll change your mind
once you see how we can control nature . . ."

"I already know how we control nature--enough
to blow the tar out of a city five times the size
of the shelter, or slaughter hundreds of people
with the flick of a wrist . . ."

Then the sharp sting of his father's
backhand.

"Don't you _ever_ talk to me that way. . . ."

#

Ian didn't really know how big unicorns
might be. He had read about them, but books
never clearly defined their size. As he
walked, he looked under rocks, examined caves
and cliffs, and sifted through rubble, as
well as kept one eye on the horizon at all
times, looking for scouts--or unicorns.

To keep from going crazy, he talked·to his
mouse.

#

"No, I can't say that I ever saw a unicorn, though surely, it's not for·a lack of
trying. I just don't think I could see
right--I don't think any of us could."

"But, rainbows, that's another story. I've
seen plenty of those in my day. They're
pretty hard to describe, though; they're real
colorful. Yeah, that's it, 'the beauty of
all colors/and all things.' I don't know any
other way to say it."

"But listen here, young man, always--always
look for the unicorns. They're waiting for
us--if we can learn to see." Then the old
man fell asleep.

Radiologist apprentice Stallworth (grade 5)
and Medical apprentice Jameson (grade 3) got
up to leave. They had heard what he said,
but didn't put much faith in the words. The
old man was supposed to be senile anyway. . . .

83

"Hey, Freddy--look over there." Ian pointed to a small dot on the horizon, "What d'ya think it is?"

The mouse didn't stir.

"Okay, go ahead and sleep. I'm going to find out."

Ian started off toward the dot with the mouse's cage in his hand. For all he knew, it could've been the search party that was sent out for him. Even so, he strode quickly and surely toward it, and his heart was light.

The mouse lifted its head lazily. "Squeak?"

"Yeah, I know what I'm doing."

#

" . . . But Ian, I can't go. As only a medical apprentice (grade 3), I have no access to zero level."

"But Freddy, I can't go without you. We both vowed that we would find the unicorns together. Don't you want to go? You've got to come."

Her eyes watered as she again turned him down. She wiped her face on the cuff of her antiseptic cloak. "But here," she handed him a covered cage, "take him along to keep you safe." In case you lose your film or something, look at him every once in a while. He'll be getting as much radiation as you. The less active he gets, the more radiation you get." She held him tight and pulled away before she got tears on his clothes. "Take care, and don't steal scout 7--it's being used for reconnaissance tomorrow."

"Don't you want to . . ."

But she had already walked off down the hall.

#

The spot disappeared long before Ian and
Freddy got there. Dejectedly, Ian sat down
by a stream that, according to his geiger
counter, was only lightly contaminated.

"Well, Freddy, what shall we do now?"

Freddy seemed to have a hard time lifting
his head. He said, "Squeak." It was a weak,
small sound.

"Yeah," Ian said, "yeah, that's easy for
you to say."

In fact, it wasn't.

#

After two days of staying near the stream,
Ian, who was sick of his own odor, and tired
of the stale air, stripped off his Rad-suit.
He saw his own skin for the first time in a
week--it was bright red. Stage I in radiation
poisoning.

In a fit of anger, Ian ripped the film out
of its socket. Still way below red-line, he
thought, I must've gotten some defective film.
He looked around for something to throw, and,
finding nothing, he sat down hard.

"Well, what do ya think of that, Freddy?"

No answer.

"Freddy?" He looked over into the mouse's
cage and saw Freddy's white form stretched
out over the bottom of the cage.

He tossed the cage into the stream, which
caught it, and swung it on a long voyage to
the sea.

"Bon Voyage," Ian said, "let me know what
it's like."

In an hour, Ian's dehydrated form lay
vomiting violently into the stream. Stage II
of radiation poisoning.

#

85

Scout 2 pulled to a stop thirty yards from the stream. Three men jumped out and covered a small distance to the immobile human body nearby.

"Yeah, this's the one," the first man said.

"My god," said the second man, "not much to take back, is there?"

"No," said the third man, toeing the body over, "grab the radiation suit and let's go--wait a minute, what's this?" He bent and picked up a small notebook.

"Must be his diary," the first man sneered, "might as well chunk it."

"No," said the second man, "it's s'posed to go to next of kin."

"Yeah," said the third man, "but old man Stallworth's had enough embarrassment to last him a life-time. Send it to Writer/Poet Fredericks."

"Sure thing," said the second man, "let's get home. I don't like this place."

#

6/24/3434

Well,they've come. They were here just a little while ago, although I wouldn't have known it from the way they've been messed up. The whole metabolism must not be anything like ours--they mutated quickly, and they're uglier than hell.

They don't have horns. Not a single one had a horn on its head. And none of them were white. They were all sick grey or brown, or black. The closest any of them came was the one that had a dirty white coat overlaid with big brown splotches.

And all their tails were messed up. They were frayed rather than straight. And they weren't long enough.

We've screwed everything up.

Even so, I still think they're beautiful. That's where you in the shelter, and I disagree.

I could sit here to watch them forever, if I wasn't about to die.

You wouldn't even see the beauty.

From The Memoirs of Ian Stallworth, six months as number one bestseller. Published Posthumously by Unicorn Press.

--Eric Coleman
10th Grade

THE WHITE PRINCESS, THE GOLD PRINCESS, AND THE BLACK HAIRED MINSTREL

The land of Silvan lay stretched between the Assisilus Mountains and the Lake of Pergodus. It was a fertile land, unspoiled, and was known far and wide for its fine and different crops. Most of Silvan's fame came from the fact that everything, including the citizens, were brightly colored. There were no greys or blacks in Silvan; only the brightest colors were allowed there. It was law.

The color rule was made by the White Princess. It was the only law she ever passed, and was a strange one at that, because the Princess and her friends were devoid of any color.

The White Castle was nestled between the Assisilus Mountains. It was made of ivory and polished so brightly that the sparkle of the sun upon its surface could blind the innocent onlooker. The castle was surrounded by a thirty foot ivory wall, patrolled by a number of white guard dogs.

Inside, the princess wandered about alone. She was indeed white, with a mass of long, straight, almost silver hair. She was beautiful, with her tall, thin form and delicate features. The only spot of color ever near the princess was her eyes.

They were large, liquid and aquamarine.

She was always alone, wandering about her rooms. She did play her music, on a white flute. No one in the village knew why the princess kept to herself, and there was much gossip about her seclusion. Once, it was said, some adventurous

87

village boys had climbed up to the castle windows and looked in on the princess. It was also said that they were never seen again.

On the opposite end of Silvan, by the side of the Pergodus Lake, stood the Gold Castle. It was originally made of pure gold, but its princess had long since chipped off the surface metal to give to the peasants. Afterwards, the castle was made of wood and polished until it was golden in color.

The princess was always seen running barefoot about the village, her blonde curly hair swinging behind her. She wore only peasant clothes, unlike the silks and satins of the White Princess.

The two princesses knew of each other, vaguely, but neither had any desire to visit the other. They had lived this way--one alone, wandering through her empty castle, and one always surrounded by villagers, running through the streets, for as long as either could remember.

Meanwhile, in the center of Silvan, a young minstrel was talking with a small group of peasants.

"How long do you plan to stay?" a grubby, smiling boy asked.

"Till I leave," replied the musician. He strummed his lute. The group of people fell silent, straining to catch every note of his hypnotic music.

When he had finished, the same boy again sidled up to him and asked, "Have you heard of the White Princess?"

"No, tell me," answered the minstrel.

So the boy told him about the princess, the castle, and the rumors about the dangers of going there.

"I think I'll go see her," the minstrel said. The villagers stared open-mouthed as he stood up, picked up his lute, and headed towards the Assisilus Mountains.

Once the minstrel reached the mountains, he sat down to watch the castle guard dogs. After a few minutes he had learned the patterns of the patrolling dogs and at the time between their crossings, he slipped in and scaled the wall. Once inside he found a high, tiny ladder leading to one of the castle windows. He slowly made his way up the ladder, struggling with his instrument.

The windows in the white castle were very high up, as the minstrel soon found, and were made of a strange sort of milky-white glass. As the minstrel reached out to touch them, he noticed that his hand came away sticky. For an unknown reason, the minstrel licked his hand. His eyes twinkled. Of course, it was made from sugar.

It was practically made to break into noiselessly," the minstrel mused to himself.

He began to eat his way through the spun-sugar pane. When he had made his way through the window, he found himself inside a large circular room. The walls, ceiling and floor were white. Huge white pillows lay scattered about. A few white persian cats ran in and out of the towers of cushions.

From outside in the hall came a soft swishing sound. The musician hid behind one of the larger pillows. He peeked around a corner. The swishing became louder, and the princess entered the room. The minstrel drew in his breath.

She was indeed as beautiful as the villagers had told him. Her long satin skirt made more soft sounds as she moved. She gracefully settled in among the pillows and began to play her lute.

The minstrel began to play along with her. At the sound of his music, she sat up, dropping her instrument.

"Who is it?" she said in a deep, cold voice.

The minstrel came out, still playing. He smiled his most warm and flirtatious smile, a smile that was known to win over the market girls.

"Hello," he said.

"You are not welcome here," the princess said, her aquamarine eyes turning icy. She looked at his instrument. "What is that you have?" "My lute, dear princess. Same as yours." The minstrel continued playing. The princess closed her eyes, "You may play for a time," she said.

The minstrel left the white castle many hours later, his fingers aching from the effort of playing.

The princess had not spoken again after giving him permission to stay, and had dismissed him by standing up some hours later, and walking from the room.

She was cold, hard, and very beautiful. He knew he loved her; the way she played, her grace and her calm. But he also knew that she was quite untouchable.

With this on his mind he began once again to cross the land of Silvan. On his way he heard talk of the Gold Princess. Deciding at once to meet her also, he headed for the Gold Castle, but he found her in the marketplace. She was running about in her peasant skirts and bare feet. She ran up to him at once, seeing that he was a newcomer and hugged and kissed him.

He was invited to the castle where he played for some of the villagers. Everyone but the princess sat still. The princess ran about, laughing and talking. She would sit still listening for about a minute and then she was running away again.

After a few hours, the minstrel asked to be excused and wandered outside to think things over.

He knew he loved the Gold Princess. She was warm and loving, but flighty. The White Princess was just the opposite--cold, unfeeling, but graceful, calm. While he sat, waiting for an answer to come to him, an old, crippled villager came up to him.

"What are you troubled by, young man?" the peasant croaked, settling down beside the minstrel.

"Wondering, grandfather."

"About what?"

"Oh, the princesses."

"Ah, yes," said the peasant. "Many young men have 'wondered,' shall we say, over the princesses!" he chuckled. "Play me a song, minstrel, and then I'll tell you their story."

So the minstrel played again, hurriedly, for he was eager to hear about the two.

After he had finished and the old man had awakened from the hypnotic trance that the music had put him in, the story was told.

"You see," said the old man. "The princesses are the same person. Don't look so amazed, it's true. They were separated at birth--split into two different people by the witch who killed the King and Queen. She was horrible, that witch. Ugly old thing." He hawked and spat on the ground. "Young man, many have tried to bring them back together. Nothing helps."

At once the musician knew what to do. He jumped up. "I know! I know exactly!" he said.

For the next three months, he stayed in the forest, catching game and drinking stream water. When he was ready he collected the Gold Princess and set off for the White Castle. The princess was very excited at the prospect of adventure and laughed and jumped about as they walked.

They reached the White Castle in two days and nights. The minstrel demonstrated how to sneak in and the princess soon followed him.

They found themselves inside the same circular room. Instantly, the white princess swished in angrily.

"Get out," she said in a threatening voice. "Get out."

This was his cue; the minstrel began playing the song he had worked on for those three months. Every note said something and he played his love for them with each strain.

He looked down, only once, at his hands, and when he looked up again, the princesses were gone.

Instead, in their place stood a new girl.
She had the curly blonde hair of the Gold
Princess and the white skin of the White
Princess. She was not beautiful, but her smile
shone out at him and she seemed to be radiantly
alive. She walked up to the minstrel and
kissed him.

"Thank you," she said.

--Cathy Cain
10th Grade

That might be as far as you want to go with
fairy tales--but then you might choose to go just one
step further. Here it is: Would you be curious
about how your fairy tale might be interpreted?
Hmmm . . . I thought so! Carl Jung, a psychologist
who has spent most of his life studying the meaning
of fairy tales and dreams, suggests the following
broad guidelines for interpreting your own fairy
tales.

1. Look at all of the characters in your
   fairy tale and examine their relationships
   to each other. These characters are all
   aspects of your own personality and psyche,
   all a part of you. Can you recognize yourself in them?

2. The setting of your tale is probably symbolic of at least some aspect of your present
   emotional "locale"--that is, a place you
   fear, or a place you wish to be, etc.

3. The conflict of the story is probably a
   symbolic representation of some conflict you
   are currently experiencing, have experienced
   in the past but haven't resolved satis-
   factorily, or are afraid of experiencing in
   the future.

4. The ending you chose for your fairy tale is
   probably the least significant aspect of the
   interpretation, and its interpretation
   depends largely on how you interpret the other
   three elements of the tale.

If you wish to have more information about
Jung's theory of the interpretation of fairy tales,
consult: Marie Louise Von Franz, Interpretation of
Fairy Tales and Carl Jung, Man and His Symbols.

Keep in mind that Jung points out that over-generalization in interpretation is very risky, that only you can really "make sense" of your own fairy tale. Don't take it too seriously; try Jung's theory and just see if it says anything to you about yourself and your life right now; look at it as an experiment--not a fact! Enjoy! What do you think?

Exercise 2: Create Your Own Fantasy: Go ahead . . . just cut loose and fantasize--no limitations, no restrictions, no "process" or steps to follow . . . just write out one of your fantasies. Below are some student samples of poems that were written out of this exercise of simply fantasizing freely. The first is entitled "Narnia", a reference to C. S. Lewis', "Narnia":

NARNIA

Into this other world
I creep sometimes,
Passing through the silver door
Of the full length mirror
Into a world
            of witches, rings, and lions . . .
Under hems of suspended skirts
            and watchful shirtcuffs--
Breathing rose sachet and mothballs.

I must shift all the shoes
          to the corner
To make room
         For this overgrown child.
I huddle
      knees to my chest.

Except for the thin strip of light
Seeping through the door crack
It is black, the comforting darkness
of aloneness.

Crowded now
My legs are too long
For extended hiding time.
But in this secret closet
Magic still lingers--
The clothes hang silently
And can keep secrets.

                --Karen King
                12th Grade

I WANNA DROWN

Come lay me down in Elysian fields
We'll make ourselves gentle in chaos
swallow me in your wetness
(the sea comes in on a million small hooves)
your skin, white as foam
(you embrace the shore)
my arms around you as brown as the sand
your mouth, sweet, warm.

Come sleep in my bed of anarchy
(in the sea, each wave a stallion)
we rode the beach, you a chestnut, me a roan,
then slept in drowsy discord.
When you wake up you'll leave me
(like the tide, you return)
and I smile, back in the city
my mouth tasting of salt.

                              --Bill Johnston
                              11th Grade

ON THE EXISTENCE OF GODDESSES

I once dreamed of a beautiful goddess,
Found wandering the Olympian landscape,
To whom even Olympus, in all its grandeur,
    existed as but a subtle backdrop.
Whose music has soothed the savage beast.
Whose hair, the sun's own golden mane,
    has blinded all her foes.
Who walked freely among endless
    Medusaes and Minotaurs.
And she felt no fear.

I once dreamed of a beautiful goddess
Who saddled Pegasus,
    and stumped the Sphinx
With her wit.
Whose utterance could send an army to war,
    and then bring them home again.
And, when the blood had been shed,
    whose smile stood proof that
Beauty had not been lost.
And she could not hate.

But goddesses no longer wander my dreams.
I'm told they don't exist--
                    never have.

But I know better.
I have seen a goddess

```
                         (she has no Pegasus)
Who sings and
          plays a guitar
                    (never even seen the Sphinx)
With blond hair and
          green eyes
                  (wouldn't send anyone to war)
Her smile stands proof
               that beauty is not lost
                    (She must feel fear)
And, I find dreaming is no longer necessary,
     because goddesses
                    do exist.

                    --Eric Coleman
                      10th Grade
```

PRETTY DANCER

Pretty Dancer comes to
You with flowers in her smile
And sweet baby's breath
For your soft lips.

She comes floating on
Lamp-like clouds of fantasy
Bringing faint perfume of
Some unknown flickering mirage.

The willowy spring grass
Wavers in the wind,
Hesitant, like Pretty Dancer,
Waiting for the wind's soft invitation.

Lifting her head she pirouettes--
A leaf trickling graciously
From majestic heavens,
To rest in the splendor of your shade.

Touch Pretty Dancer gently,
Caress the songs of her imaginings
And kiss, ever so softly,
The violets in her eyes.

```
                    --Elizabeth Plaag
                      12th Grade
```

Hopefully, these imagination exercises will establish a mood, set a pattern for seeing and expressing yourself in new ways--and warm you up--to your imagination, your creativity, your rich world of the right brain.

95

FOOTNOTES: CHAPTER IV

[1]Edward De Bono, Lateral Thinking (New York: Harper Colophon Books, 1970), 9.

[2]De Bono (1970), 9-14, 39-45.

[3]C. Hugh Holman, ed., A Handbook to Literature (Indianapolis: Bobbs-Merrill Educational Publishing, 1980), 225.

[4]William Shakespeare, A Midsummer Night's Dream, quoted in Walter McBee, Writer's Journal: Explorations (Dallas: Harcourt Brace Jovanovich, Inc., 1972), 117.

[5]The following discussion of Shakespeare's definition of "strong imagination" is an adaptation from Walter McBee, Writer's Journal: Explorations, 117-120.

[6]Beverly Galyean, "The Brain, Intelligence and Education" Implications for Gifted Programs," Position Paper presented to the State Department of Education, Division of Gifted and Talented (January, 1981), 4.

[7]Galyean, 4; also supported by the research of Leslie Hart, How the Brain Works (New York: Basic Books, 1975); Jeanne Chall and Allan Mirsky, eds., Education and the Brain. The Seventy-Seventh Yearbook of the National Society for the Study of Education, Part 2 (Chicago, University of Chicago Press, 1978), 308-342; Paul D. MacLean, "A Meeting of Minds," Dromenon: A Journal of New Ways of Being, 3 (1980), 12-19; Carl Sagan, The Dragons of Eden (New York: Ballantine, 1977).

[8]Thomas Blakeslee, "Your Unconscious Dreamy Brain: It's All Right, Research Finds," Science Digest (July, 1980), 36.

[9]Blakeslee, 36.

[10]Galyean, 8.

[11]An adaptation of "Education of the Self," Exercises in Harold C. Lyon, Learning to Feel--Feeling

to Learn (Columbus, OH: Charles E. Merrill Publishing
Co., 1971), 134.

CHAPTER V

SYNECTICS:
BEYOND PETER BELL--OR THE ART OF
PERCEIVING RELATIONSHIPS

Have you ever heard of Peter Bell? (Poor
ole Peter Bell?) William Wordsworth describes him
this way: "A primrose by the river's brim was but
a primrose to him."

Peter Bell had single vision. He was so
bound to the "real," physical left brain world that
he had lost, or never had developed, his higher
powers of vision. He saw only what his eyes could
see, only with his physical senses. He had cut
himself off from his right brain powers and was left
with no insight (no sight within), no imagination.
He was uncentered.

Hopefully, after the last chapter of working
to develop and to trust your imagination, you are not
in danger of being a Peter Bell. But let's take a
final step. Let's concentrate on a crucial aspect
of imagination and creativity--the art of perceiving
things in new, fresh, original relationships. Remember that, in Chapter IV, the point was made that the
power to inner relationships is a key to understanding
imagination. Also, this power of seeing the interrelatedness of things is a key to dealing with our
experience imaginatively, to perceiving the significance of what we are experiencing, and to centering.
In fact, it is this attunement and balance of the
physical senses with imagination that opens the door
to the interrelatedness of things, to our ability to
perceive inner relationships.

Marilyn Ferguson, in her excellent book The
Aquarian Conspiracy, discusses a new field of psychology, synectics, which deals with the process of
thinking metaphorically, of making connections and
perceiving relationships.[1] Obviously, a metaphor
or symbol is a natural bridge between the hemispheres,
for symbols symbolically carry knowledge from the
non-verbal right brain, which stores knowledge in
images, metaphors and symbols, to the left brain where
it is recognized as being like something already
stored there. Hence, metaphorical thinking tends to

speed up the bridging process between right and
left hemispheres.

Many educators, psychologists, and brain
researchers agree that perhaps the greatest disability
of our mental processes is pattern-blindness, the
inability to see relationships or detect meaning from
large bodies of information, the ability to make
wholes from disparate parts, to see the interredlated-
ness of things.

Brain research has found that people perceived to be "highly intelligent" possess the ability
to engage in increasingly more complex patterns of
thinking.[2]   Yet each of us houses the apparently innate
ability in the right hemisphere to think in gestalts,
to intuitively grasp spontaneous and sudden flashes
of insight and understanding. One way of tapping
that resource, of developing that natural ability
of pattern-seeing is through synectics, or metaphorical thinking. This chapter provides many
approaches to and practical applications of the art
of perceiving relationships.

Tapping the Mind's Natural Flow: Free Association

Modern psychology tells us that the act of
perceiving inner relationships is a natural process:
that it occurs involuntarily, without our "willing"
it or "making" it happen; that it cannot be avoided,
in fact. Most of us, however, do not consciously
observe our associations. Although psychologists
generally agree on very little, most do concur that
learning is the formation of associations between
our experience (physical stimuli) and our responses
to it. Gestalt psychologists view our awareness of
these associations as one factor which leads us to
new patterns of thought, or insight.

It is obvious, then, why writers often use
the "free association" technique to stimulate their
writing. Let's try some "free association" exercises
and see if it opens any doors of understanding for
you about how your mind works, about associations
you've unconsciously formed. But first, what is
the "free association" technique? The concept of
free association is based on several premises: (1) The
mental-emotional life is illogical, unorganized and
disorderly, disjointed, and intuitive. (2) The
major patterning of the mental life of the ordinary

100

person is _associative_, that is, marked by the mental linking of objects or events which have been encountered in juxtaposition, rather than logical. This psychological association is one of the chief processes forming our emotional attitudes and values toward the external world. For example, participation in a train wreck might cause a person to forever associate train whistles with fear; or a loved one's pipe tobacco or perfume reminds him/her of the loved one, or a particular experience with the loved one. (3) There is a merging of time in the mind; everything is "now". An external event happening this moment is presented in the mind simultaneously with all of the associations and feelings and recollections it arouses. James Joyce described it this way: "The past is consumed in the present and the present is living only because it brings forth the past."

Do you understand the concept of free association? If so, let's try working with it.

Exercise 1 - Free Association with Words:

Step 1.: You will be given a series of words. Take one word at a time, and write in columns under each word your associations with it. Write every word or phrase that comes immediately to your mind. Express every idea, sensation, feeling, fantasy, or thought that occurs to you, no matter how insignificant, irrelevant, shameful or silly it might seem. In short, write quickly without censoring yourself. No one else will see your list. Below is the list of words you are to use in this association exercise.

red	wave
snore	window
winter	mother

Step 2: Now, with a friend or in a small group setting, share your list aloud, leaving off any words you don't want to read. Notice how differently each person responds to the same word. How do you explain this, knowing what you do about free association? Notice, too, that there is no "right" or "wrong" response.

Step 3: Next examine your associations to one word in the list. Consider your responses in the light of each of the premises of free association. Can you see a pattern or patterns in your associations?

Does any of it make sense to you? Did one association trigger another? Were there any surprises for
you, any associations that were unexpected?

Step 4: Many writers use the free association technique to stimulate their ideas and writing
habits. Have you ever "been blocked"? Just felt
you couldn't write, or had no ideas to write about?
Try free association--something always happens.

However, the raw material, the free associations as you've listed them, won't make any sense
to anyone but you, and perhaps they don't make much
sense to you. How do you go about turning that into
a poem or a story? Obviously you can't lay your
associations on the reader in that pure, raw form.
You must first find a pattern of meaning your associations have for you; then you must intellectualize,
that is, organize your responses. Here is a fun way
to introduce yourself to this process: Take one of
the words you wrote associative responses to and try
writing a sentence, or even a poem with some or all
of the words on your list in it. Following are some
student responses that were produced in response to
the word grandfather:

GRANPA'S SCALES

My first fish! I never caught one so big
before! Granpa says I can keep it. He weighs
it in his hands. His hands have spots on them.
Brown spots. Cancer . . . is it brown? He
takes his knife out and scales the fish. It's
like shaving. Granpa doesn't shave. He leaves
his whiskers on. It scratches when he kisses
my cheek. I hope I can't catch cancer like a
cold. I don't want to have anything growing
inside of me like Granpa does. They say it's
in his colon. We learned about a semi-colon
last week in school. I wish the cancer was
there instead. The fish is green. Maybe
cancer's green. Most things that grow are green.
Maybe if I swallow the fish, I'll have cancer.
Then I can go where Granpa goes. He's cutting
the belly open. They will pull his insides out.
I don't want cancer! I don't want to be cut
up like the fish! Granpa doesn't want to either.
He says, "I want to be whole when my time comes."
The blood spills out of the belly. I want to
put the insides back in and sew it up. I want
it to be whole.

"It's a beauty of a fish!" Granpa says.
No, please don't kiss me, Granpa. Your scales
hurt my face. . . .

--Debbie Gardner
12th Grade

MASTERPIECE

Lines
Drawn
One
By one
Over the years
Twist, turn
Deepen, widen
And shift
With emotions
On a round
Brown canvas.
The artist is
Time,
Your face--
A masterpiece.

--Karen E. King
12th Grade

STREAM OF CONSCIOUSNESS

The moon could be seen rising over the lake
and pine trees like a beautifully driven
golf ball . . . the fireplace was lit because
my sister was ten and had taken firebuilding
in girlscouts and we roasted marshmallows
together and ate them by the bagful. I was
eight and we often were alone in the cabin.
The fish we had caught smelled loudly (still on
the hook in the sink) and we were proud and happy
and acted out Sonny and Cher songs; we had white
go-go boots. Then we sang Mr. Moon, Moon, bright
and shining moon hiding behind that tree--Oh how
I'd like to love ya but I gotta run cause there's
a man behind me with a Big Shot Gun . . .! But it
was late and nobody came so we went to bed in the
built-in bunks. I woke up to gold clubs banging
on the floor and Dad and the other men roared
in laughing and the ice started clinking and fish
flying. We pulled the covers over our heads
hoping he'd forget we were there but he didn't
forget me. He dragged me out of bed and slop-
pily carried me in the living room and dumped

me on the couch. And all these eyes stared
at me like the dead fish in the sink and they
put Nancy Sinatra in the Comet stereo and
made me act out "These Boots are Made for
Walking" and I wanted to run into the dark
away from them but they caught me up in their
arms and threw me up in the air the cow jumped
over the moon--a glass broke and shattered
broken moonbeams and whiskey over the lake.
I ran and hid up in the top bunk, this time
a princess in the black knight's tower.

--Karen E. King
12th Grade

THE FUNERAL

Sprays of white, red, pink, and orange
Flowers
Fill the room.
Sprinkles of purple and
Yellow are splashed throughout,
Making the black wooden box
That they cover
Even darker.
And in that dark box
A face of steel
Melts to sleet
and fog
Then stands stagnant
And icy.

--Julianne Parsons
11th Grade

Notice that for some of these responses the pattern
of association that emerged was a memory that was
expanded; for some it was a series of descriptive
images or sense impressions.

O.K.? Are you ready to try it? Have fun!

Exercise 2 - Sound Associations: Actually you could
do this exercise with any of the five senses, but
let's try sound. Below are a series of words. Under
each word, list sounds the words suggest to you:

      spaghetti   flower

        train   gun

Isn't that weird? Have you ever really thought about
the sounds you associate with a flower--or spaghetti--
or a gun? Look especially closely at your responses
that are surprising to you and different from your

friend's associations. Now, again, try to organize
to intellectualize your responses by forming a pattern
and making a poem. Below is a poem that developed
from the word gun:

THE UNOFFICIAL VERSION

The cannon blows, echoes through the canyon walls
                                 the canyon walls
                                    summer falls
                           the children sleep
                                        unaware
                              soldiers there
                            under the trees
                         a pillow of leaves
                           the general bellows
                         the sun breaks yellow
                            the soldiers roar
                               asleep no more
                                sounds of war
                           the children wake
                           the branches break
                             clarions crying
                               dying, dying
                               wall of fire
                              higher, higher
                              burn them down

                           now nothing left but
                                        ground.

                          --David McLaughlin
                             11th Grade

        All right . . . so much for free association,
for now, anyway. Obviously Peter Bell wasn't conscious
of his associations, or a primrose would have been
much more interesting to him! Now let's look at some
ways of using our natural flow of associations to take
us beyond Peter Bell vision and to help us perceive
our primroses, our physical world in fresh, original
ways.

Perceiving Relationships Between the
Real and the Abstract

        One reason ole Peter had single vision is that
he did not "see" beyond the physical, "real" world.
He ignored the world of abstractions . . . maybe you
do, too. How would you define abstraction? A simple
way of putting it is that abstractions are ideas,
concepts, and emotions which are apart from concrete,
physical existence. That is not to say that

abstractions are not "real" or that they do not exist; they simply cannot be physically or scientifically observed. Name some abstractions . . . Love? Loneliness? Fear? Peace? Worry? You see, the effects--or results--of abstractions are physically observable, but not the idea itself. Love is abstract, but an act of love, such as a kiss, physically observable--and (we might add) enjoyable!

Writers often need and want to write about abstractions, yet because they are not physical and concrete, we all have different associations about their meaning. For example, have you ever compared your idea of what God is with someone else's? Or love? Or patriotism? To prove a point, try this exercise:

Exercise 3 - Definition Poems:

Step 1: Write down as many definitions as you can come up with the abstraction home. Now, by reading your definitions aloud in a group or to a friend, compare your definition with that of others. See how very difficult it is to define an abstraction.

Step 2: The only way to clearly communicate what an abstraction really means to you is to describe it in the most concrete terms you can. To give you practice, let's go back to the use of the free association technique. Following are some abstractions: worry, fear, pleasure, time, friendship. Choose one of those abstractions, or one of your own selection not listed here, and list concrete things you associate with that abstraction. How does it feel, taste, smell, look, sound? What experience, memories, objects is it associated with in your mind?

Step 3: Now write a definition poem, defining that abstraction by listing or cataloguing its concrete, physical qualities. Below are two student samples. Notice that the first is simply a series of images, especially sensory experiences, which are "catalogued", to use Whitman's term:

HUMILIATION

Humiliation is
    the taste of sharp metal in your mouth,
    stinging, cold, and soon to be swallowed
    to churn in your stomach.

It is
    the prickling of a thousand pins all over
    your face as the blood rises to its call.

the sound of mocking laughter, and whispers
heard by everyone but you.
Humiliation is
the scratchy touch of a worn wool coat
given you by the women's charity committee.
It is the sight of the predator's moving mouth,
and everyone has turned to watch with
laughing faces.
Humiliation is the smell of your shirt sleeve
as you bury your face in it

the loudness of your pencil on paper as you
pretend
to concentrate on school work
It is the sound of your mutant words
falling out like lead bricks because
you've just learned a new language
Humiliation is
the sin
of becoming the prey
instead of one of the hunters.

--Lisi Cocina
10th Grade

TIME-TANGLES

I thought to keep my self a secret;
But I was wrong--
For Time is not silent.
Snarled and screaming,
It is a blind man's tapestry
of harlequin threads--
Angel-white, bitter black,
Solitary gray and sharp sweet green--
Interwoven again
And again;
An endless spider's web
Of unspoken hopes
And regretted words;
And when threads take unsudden twists--
Distorting the unconscious pattern--
Or pull taut
In the unbearable tension
Of counted heartbeats,
They snap--
Hang limp, and unanchored,
Drift to drowning fog.
But the spiders
Still weave
The time-tangles
Still scream--

And secret selves are
Hidden crimson threads

--Juliet Lee
11th Grade

Now study this professional poem by Robert
Hershon. It defines horror through vivid, strong
concrete images.

ON HORROR

If it is horrible to be burned alive by savage
        tribesmen
who dance and leap about as your wrist watch
        melts,
                it is horrible to be burned by a hot pot.
If it is horrible in the great gothic house when
        the hairy claw
comes through the velvet drape and clutches your
        throat,
                it is horrible when your child touches
                        your hand as you sleep.
If it is horrible when the fiendish vaudevillian,
        in a rage because
you were in the fourth grade with his wife, pins
        you to the wall
with his wicked throwing knives and takes dead aim
        at your breast pocket,
                it is horrible to mince onions.
If it is horrible to be buried under an avalanche
        of snow and rocks
set off by a mad alpinist, shrieking in the thin
        air,
                it is horrible to drop a book on your toe.
If it is horrible to be drowned in the relentless
        flood as you were racing
to warn the FBI that bearded saboteurs were
        lurking near the dam,
                it is horrible to scrub your feet in the
                        bath.
But if the pot boils without heat?
If the child's eyes are dark, the infant prowling?
If the book, new to your eyes, curses your name?

There is horror in all love, in the sweet apple.
The mouth cannot taste it, the hand cannot feel it.
Horror is small and warm and damp
and wears your mother's dresses.[3]

Notice how interestingly he juxtaposes those images
to say even more through the comparison. The pattern

and structure of the poem (each section beginning with an "if" clause, followed by a contrasting image, then at the end reaching his defining images, and the last two lines bring all the contrasts together.) You might like to use this pattern as a model for your own definition poem.

<u>Exercise 4 - What Is Poetry?</u>: An abstraction that we have been toying with (or have we been <u>working</u> with it?) throughout this book is the abstract concept <u>poetry</u>. You have been writing <u>poems</u>, but what is <u>poetry</u>? That is like asking, "What is the difference between a painting and art?" Just as it seems that all touring musicians must write a song about life on the road (example: Jackson Brown's <u>Running on Empty</u>), poets seem compelled to write about poetry. Robert Frost defines poetry as "a lump in the throat, a heart-sickness, lovesickness, loneliness which cannot be said, only felt."[4]

Here are two examples of poems poets have written to define poetry through cataloguing images, associations and sensory experiences:

ARS POETICA

A poem should be palpable and mute
As a globed fruit,
Dumb
As old medallions to the thumb,
Silent as the sleeve-worn stone
Of casement ledges where moss has grown--
A poem should be wordless
As the flight of birds.

*

A poem should be motionless in time
As the moon climbs,
Leaving, as the moon releases
Twig by twig the night-entangled trees,
Leaving, as the moon behind the winter leaves,
Memory by memory the mind--
A poem should be motionless in time
As the moon climbs.

*

A poem should be equal to:
Not true.
For all the history of grief
An empty doorway and a maple leaf.

For love
The learning grasses and two lights above
   the sea--
A poem should not mean
But be. [5]

--Archibald MacLeish

POETRY IS . . . .

Poetry is a projection across silence of cadences
arranged to break that silence with definite
intentions of echoes, syllables, wave lengths.

Poetry is a journal of a sea animal living on
land, wanting to fly the air.

Poetry is a series of explanations of life,
fading off into horizons too swift for explanations.

Poetry is a search for syllables to shoot at
   barriers
of the unknown and the knowable.

Poetry is a theorum of a yellow-silk handker-
chief knotted with riddles, sealed in a balloon
tied to the tail of a kite flying in a white wind
against a blue sky in spring.

Poetry is the silence and speech between a wet
struggling root of a flower and a sunlit blossom
of that flower.

Poetry is the harnessing of the paradox of earth
cradling life and then entombing it.

Poetry is a phantom script telling how rainbows
are made and why they go away.

Poetry is the synthesis of hyacinths and biscuits.

Poetry is the opening and closing of a door;
leaving those who look through to guess about
what is seen during a moment. [6]

--Carl Sandburg

Compare your definition of poetry with these poets'
views. What does each say about how the poet feels
about poetry? For example, when Sandburg says
poetry is "a synthesis of hyacinths and biscuits,"
what is he saying about the nature of poetry?

    Instead of defining poetry through a series
of images, some poets have used one sustained developed

image.   Lawrence Ferlinghetti defines the poet as
tight-rope walker:

CONSTANTLY RISKING

Constantly risking absurdity

and death

whenever he performs

above the heads
of his
audience

the poet like an acrobat

climbs on rime
to a high wire of
his own making

and balancing on eyebeams

above a sea of faces

paces his way

to the other side of day

performing entrechats

and sleight-of-foot
tricks

and other high theatrics

and all without mistaking
any thing
for what it may not be

For he's the super realist

who must perforce perceive

taut truth

before the taking of each
stance or step

in his supposed advance

toward that still higher
perch

where Beauty stands and waits

with gravity

to start her death-
defying leap

And he

a little charleychaplin man

who may or may not
catch

her fair eternal form

spreadeagled in the
empty air

of existence[7]

--Lawrence Ferlinghetti

111

SKINNY POEM

Skinny
poem;
all
your
ribs
showing
even
without
a
deep
breath

thin
legs
rotted
with disease.

Live
here!
on
this
page,
barely
making
it,
like

the
mass
of
mankind.[8]

   --Lou Lipsitz

Another defines poetry as a tree:

THE POEM THAT TRIES TO BE A TREE

assumes it is true to put down roots,
invading land as it does the air.
Travellers for miles around
marvel at the open horizon, vapid
as all that is, and pass by.

If only for fantasy, there would be
birds if they saw it. Alone,
it is a fantasy of the pure earth,
belief in itself crass against the sky,
with twigs bent in their doing.

112

Resisting any roots, the land allows
it, ungrowable as old newspaper
in this latitude. Pushing past,
strangers to the climate see things
it is not, itself: a giant bower,

a study in ingrown longevity
resistant, as it is, to all disregard.
The circus, shrine, or promised land
still waits ahead, and what once
became a tree by its own definition
shows an edge of green, and is permanent.[9]

                    --Phillip Hey

Now are you ready to try it? Remember the key to
defining abstractions is to use very specific, concrete, sensory images. You may need to do some free
associations with the word poetry to get started.
You may wish to define poetry by cataloguing a series
of images or by developing and expanding one usage.
For your study and "inspiration", below are some
student examples to this assignment which used
Sandburg's poem as a pattern:

DEFINITIONS OF POETRY

Poetry is a long look at a face that only a
      Mother could love,
   fanciful and tedious studies into
         the rhythm of breath and the
         darkest colors of man's soul

                    --Lizlie Parsons

Poetry is the commonplace made incredible
   and the incredible made commonplace--
Poetry is heaven and hell in a cauldron of
                              dreams--

                    --Amy Chambers

Poetry is spaghetti winding itself together
   under its warm blanket of sauce--
Poetry is a leaf falling too early and dying
                                         on
   the ground without a sound--

                    --Kevin Kuykendall

Poetry is a fleeting smile,
   the blink of an eye,
         a photograph of a passing fancy,

Poetry is the weeping clownfish
    and the laughing willowtree.

                        --Cathy Read

Poetry is God beating his head
    on the wall of the universe

                    --Mark Greene

These student poems defined poetry by developing one image:

RAW MEAT

It was a cow,
a big, fat, red hereford,
and it had its own life
full of cow disappointments and cow passions
and it lived more fully than any other cow,
experimented and experienced more.
    It was more than a cow.
    It was super cow.
    And all of the other cows loved it.
            But the farmer was jealous
            and he butchered it,
            and now I am going to cook
            the raw, red meat
            of that fat, red cow.
And to me it is a poem.

                        --Charlie Moore

LEAVINGS

Flash,
    Green
Whirling colored prisms sending lasers to my
                                        soul
leaving there an afterburn of luminescence

Quiet?
Quite,
Fast
streams of glowing liquid pumping into my
                                dry heart
leaving it flooded

Poetry
Invades my most private sanctuaries
Leaving me bruised with its emotion.

                    --Charlie Moore
                    12th Grade

114

Double Vision: Perceiving Relationships
Through Comparisons

Double vision doesn't mean you see in a blur,
it means you see twice as well as you do with single
vision; you see two things in one. You see through
centered, focused, balanced vision. How does this
work? By comparing! Comparison means that you are
thinking on more than one level--double vision, seeing
the interrelatedness of things.

All good thinkers (see-ers) make comparisons
in depth. That doesn't mean you go to your room, grit
your teeth, and say to yourself: "Think deeply!
Think deeply! Be profound!" We've all tried that
method, haven't we? And we know it doesn't work.
Instead, all you need to do is compare. To compare
is to think, and to compare well is to think deeply.
Study two things for intersection points: How do
these two things connect in likeness or difference?
Find an obvious similarity, then a difference within
that similarity, then likenesses within those disimi-
larities--and then another and another--and there you
are, thinking deeply, seeing double! A thing, when
placed against something else, reveals its character.
"The thing--what it is and what it is not--is always a
combination of the present moment and the context in
which you observe, the past experience you bring with
you, and the thing itself," notes Ken MacCrorie.[10]
Ezra Pound puts it this way:

You can't judge any chemical's action
merely by putting it in with more of
itself. To know it, you have got
to know its limits, both what it
is and what it is not. What
substances are harder or softer,
what more resilient, what more
compact.[11]

And Marianne Moore asked: "Didn't Aristotle say that
it is the mark of a poet to see resemblances between
incongruous things?"[12] Enough philosophizing; let's
try putting it into practice.

Exercise 5 - Recording Comparisons: Below is an
excellent exercise from MacCrorie which will heighten
your awareness of how naturally we all make comparisons:[13]

115

Record five sensory observations that strike you vividly and that you might use as comparisons at some later date. Do not choose what you think will impress others. Choose what hits your senses and holds you, for whatever reasons.

In a sense all language is metaphorical, stands for something else. The river runs. She smiles sweetly. The river is personified. Her smile is compared to sugar. As a writer you should become aware of the dead metaphor in language so you can exploit it. In Walden Thoreau began writing this sentence, "We meet at meals three times a day, and give each other a new taste. . . ," and he remembered the metaphor in the word taste. Because he did not allow the word to become abstract in his mind, he was able to finish the sentence in this way: "of that old musty cheese that we are." You can do this, too. Suppose you say that "Aunt Helen was a plain woman." Get on that word plain. If Grandmother was hard but exciting, you might continue your sentence this way: "But Grandmother was the Rocky Mountains." When you forget the dead and hidden metaphors in the language you may compose foolish sentences. For example:

> Changing the course of a fast, deep river would normally be a lost cause, but this is one cause the North High family cannot afford to lose hold of.

This is a metaphor used by a student editor to ask others to help him form the school newspaper. In it, he forgets what he is saying and asks the readers to keep hold of a river. He should remember that water is impossible to grasp.

Here is an excerpt from a paint company's directions for using artists' colors:

> Where very thin glazes are desired, Liquitex colors mixed with the Medium may be quickly and lightly rubbed over the surface with fingers and thumb in the manner of oil glazes. On the other hand, unwanted color or glaze may be wiped off.

The writer committed a blooper in using the phrase "On the other hand." He forgot its dead metaphor. Just before that he is talking about literal fingers and thumb. Like a thousand other phrases in everyday language, "on the other hand" was once a brilliant

metaphor. Now people use it so unconsciously they need
to be jogged with the vaudeville gag: "On the other
hand--she had a wart."

Now you try it. Record at least five sensory
observations that for some reason hit your senses and
hold you. Do not think about anyone's reaction. Try
to record these observations as specifically and as
sensually as you can. Then extend each of these
observations into a statement of comparison, being
aware of the natural metaphors in our language.

Exercise 6 - Writing Haikus: We can learn much from
the ancient Oriental tradition of meditation and
contemplation. For the Oriental, contemplation is
an exercise in centering, in disciplining the mind to
think deeply--and to compare. To sit before one
lotus blossom or one branch of dogwood, to focus on
it for an hour, to give up oneself to that object is
to contemplate what is there (the lotus) with what
is not there (all the flower represents).

The Japanese haiku is based on such a comparison and is an outgrowth of this act of perceiving the
interrelatedness of things. Below is a haiku by
Kato Shuson:

In the depths of the flames
I saw how a peony
crumbles to pieces.

The comparison talks about one thing (how a peony looks
when it crumbles) in terms of another (like a flame).

This is probably sounding somewhat difficult
at this point, and it is. There is nothing "simple"
about centering or about writing haiku, even though
haiku presents a deceptively simple surface. However,
if you have ever observed anything with wonder and
awe, if you have ever reacted to the world of nature
with feeling, if you have ever seen into the heart
of the relatedness of things, and if you can count, you
can write haiku.

Here is the traditional, centuries-old
Japanese formula for haiku: The haiku is seventeen
syllables in length; these syllables are divided into
three lines as follows:

1st line: five syllables
2nd line: seven syllables
3rd line: five syllables

The heaviest influence of the haiku, and also a key to its complete appreciation, is Zen Buddhism, a philosophy which leaves the mind uncluttered and goes to the unseen truth (reality) of things. Japanese Zen has been explained very simply this way:

> First, it is a fundamental point that in Japanese Zen, men and Nature are not seen in opposition, since man is part of Nature or part of the Buddha--reality. To see a frog leaping into a pond is to reel at one with it in its diving, to be for a moment feeling the same motions as the frog is thought to feel. One merges with the pond, then frog, and finally the water sound. The Japanese contemplate beautiful things-- cherry blossoms, pine branches, field-flowers-- in a meditative way that allows the object to absorb and possess the perceiver. This is the Zen philosophy. Or to take an example from such a sport as archery, one does not "master" the handsome bow and shoot the arrow; the arrow shoots itself from the bow. In the tea ceremony, one performs the beautiful ritual ás in an aesthetic dream having the dimensions of eternity. Zen, with its sense of cosmic unity and its immediate aesthetic response to reality, fortifies these attitudes.[15]

Although the compression of thought and form makes haiku the world's shortest poetry, the haiku is nevertheless able to express in miniature a full scene and a wide variety of impressions. In this economical form, the poet makes only a suggestion; the imagination of the hearer or reader must fill in the outlines. Along with his brief sketch, the poet also suggests a feeling which calls forth in the reader a responding feeling. Scant though the sketch may be, the reader fills in the remainder of the picture or scene with his own mental image, and thus recollects a full, complete picture, rich in detail and expressing a wide range of feelings.

Hints for writing good haiku:

a. The magic lies in the power of suggestions. The poem portrays a moment of vivid perception of the interrelatedness of two things.

Think of a pebble tossed into a still
pool; the impact of the haiku on the mind
should also be the same'. As we read the
haiku, it ripples across our imagination,
expanding and developing as we sense and
share the experience of the poet.

b. Some haiku are purely humorous or descriptive;
most, however, are but "fleeting responses or
impressions which illuminate the poet's awareness . . . of the identity of life on different
planes."[16]

In the Buddhist doctrine, "all things and
creatures in this world are temporary mani-
festations risen from the eternal, infinite
ocean of Life," and "everything from a
mountain peak to a cherry blossom, from a
beautiful woman to a little bird, is a part
of the universal and interrelated brotherhood
of creation."[17]

c. Write the haiku in the present tense.

d. Excellent translations and comments on haiku
are ample, among them: Zen Buddhism by Peter
Pauper Press; Harold Henderson's An Introduction to Haiku; and Haiku in English by
Charles E. Tuttle Co. Recent poets who have
shown mastery of haiku in English are Gary
Snyder, Richard Brautigan, Wallace Stevens,
and James Hackett.

Before trying your own haiku, study the following Japanese haiku.[18] Do not expect them to tell
you everything, to be a complete or even a clear
statement. Remember--the magic is in suggestion and
you, as a reader, must add to the words your own
associations, imagery, sense of interrelatedness and
perception. You thus become a co-creator in the poem.

You turn and suddenly
    There is purpling autumn sky . . .
White Fumiami!

                    --Onitsura

Broken, and broken
    Again on the sea, the moon
So easily mends.

                    --Chosu

Poor crying cricket!
   Perhaps your little husband
Was caught by our cat.

                    --Kikaku

Pine tree silhouette
   Painted by the harvest moon
On a shining sky.

                    --Ransetsu

Frog-school competing
   with lark-school softly at dusk
In the art of sound.

                    --Skiki

Twilight, whipporwill . . .
   Whistle on, sweet deepener
of dark loneliness.

                    --Basho

So cold are the waves
   The rocking gull can scarcely
Fold itself to sleep.

                    --Basho

Mirror pond of stars . . .
   Suddenly a summer shower
Dimples the water.

                    --Sora

As mountain shadows
   Darken my gate, the temple deer
Still see sun-rays.

                    --Buson

One perfect moon
   And the uncountable stars
Drowned in a green sky.

                    --Shiki

   Step 1: A Group Haiku. An effective and
enjoyable way to begin writing haiku is as a group.
A good stimulus for this activity is a photograph
of a nature scene, presented to the group in a slide,
photo-transparency or on the overhead projector.
Before writing, the group should look closely at the
details in the picture and then begin describing the
scene with compressed, precise phrases.

Next, pool all of the lists of phrases on the board, adding new descriptions until there is a large number to choose from. At this point, the group needs to note the ideas and impressions about the scene and sum up what feelings their phrases seem to reflect as a group.

The group might need to review the requirements of the haiku form, then for the actual writing process, divide the class into smaller groups of 5-7 per group. Each small group should work independently of the others--and for a sense of mystery and surprise, secretly. Each group should select one phrase from the list with which they want to begin their haiku. The group will then have to modify the phrase until it contains the correct number of syllables for the first line. The writing of the second and third lines can be done in the same way as the first, with increasing care being taken to include only those phrases and images that will convey the dominent idea or impression suggested by the scene. The fun comes in comparing the different versions of haiku that come from the master list.

Step 2: Writing Haiku Independently. Now try creating haiku entirely on your own. For stimuli for writing, you might want to stick with photographs or, like the Japanese, sit before an object of nature and contemplate its nature and its relation to your world or experience, or simply exercise your sense awareness and imagination.

Then, to begin writing, make your own list of images; this process will help bring the scene sharply into focus in your mind. Then fit these images into the haiku formula and requirements.

Below are some student haiku you might enjoy. Compare them to the haiku requirements, both in form and content, and determine which you feel are the most effective.

Reckless veil of brine
Heedless of dark jagged rocks,
Rushes toward shore.

                              --Juliet Lee
                              10th Grade

Black devouring night
Stretches hungrily, trying
To swallow the sun.

                    --Juliet Lee
                      10th Grade

Summer breeze tickling,
    caressing my thighs--lover
with twilight fingers

                    --Daloma Armentrout
                      12th Grade

Atop the candle
    the flame flickers with my heart--
two, so much alike

                    --Daloma Armentrout
                      12th Grade

Haiku: Reactions to Experience. The traditional
haiku deals with nature, but more and more, the haiku
is being used to express our feelings and reactions
to all of our experience.

        Below is an exercise first conducted at the
Learning Theatre at the University of Massachusetts
and adapted as a stimulus for haiku.[19] You might
want to try it.

        Step 1: Select a partner and get into a
space where you will not be distracted.

        Step 2: Communicate with your partner with-
out speaking by first, only touching hands, and
second, sitting back to back. Give about two minutes
to each type of communication.

        Step 3: Write haiku reacting to that experi-
ence. The following haiku were written by students
at the Learning Theatre as a result of this exercise:

Uncertain moving
Groping for understanding
Everything feeling

A warming pulse beat
Our fingers and hands entwine--
Sudden belonging

Without words we speak
    Understanding and soothing--
I think I know you

Two lives together
Under one sky in one world
Forever at war

I know I couldn't
hoping, wiggling, loving,
reach over the wall

To touch is to sense
The inner conflict of self--
I know your battle.

American Versions of the Haiku: The Tanka and the Cinquain:

The tanka and the cinquain, American versions of the haiku, attempt to do everything a haiku does in content; that is, the emphasis is still on precise, sharp images which, through the power of suggestion, expand our awareness of the interrelatedness and unity of our world. What has been altered from the haiku is the formula, and the change evolved primarily out of the differences between the Japanese and English language structures. Below is the formula for the tanka:

Formula for the Tanka:

1. Contains five unrhymed lines

2. Contains 31 syllables in the following arrangement:

   line 1: 5 syllables
   line 2: 7 syllables
   line 3: 5 syllables
   line 4: 7 syllables
   line 5: 7 syllables

Here are some samples of student tankas. Study them and see if you can identify tanka characteristics in both content and form:

Slanted streams of light
Filter into my shaded
Past. Purified dreams
Hold meetings under the tree--
Rapt in green-fold reveries

--Elizabeth Plaag
11th Grade

I envied the gulls--
Their wild cries tore at my heart.
My yearning eyes strained
To follow their carefree flight:
I wished my own chains on them.

--Juliet Lee
10th Grade

My love is like the
Wings of a big butterfly--
And on them, you must
Lie. Then both of us will find
A rose on which we can nest.

--Carolyn Haynes
12th Grade

Window-glass mirror
Reflecting that staring face
Allows no entry,
No lasting picture of warmth
Or invitation to stay.

--Missy Fieldler
12th Grade

The frozen faces,
Locked into forever smiles
(silent moment), are
Captured for eternity
Like insects in amber wood.

--Carolyn Hudson
12th Grade

Exercise 7 - Writing a Tanka: Do you get the idea?
You will find the tanka gives you a bit more freedom
and room to work in than the highly compressed haiku.
Now you try writing <u>at least</u> three tankas.

Formula for the Cinquain: Study the two
short poems below. One, "The Warning", is a word cinquain and the other, "November Night", is a syllable
cinquain. The cinquain is another American variation
of the Japanese haiku. It forces the writer to con-
dense his view of his subject into an impression/
suggestion by comparison.

NOVEMBER NIGHT

Listen . . .
With faint dry sound,
Like steps of passing ghosts,

The leaves frost crisp'd, break from the trees
And fall.

THE WARNING

Just how,
Out of the strange
Still dusk . . . as strange, as still
A white moth flew. Why am I grown
    so cold?

Traits of cinquains:

1. Both have five unrhymed lines.
2. The word cinquain ("Warning") has an arrangement of words per line: 2-4-6-8-2
3. The syllable cinquain ("November Night") has
   an arrangement of syllables per line:
   2-4-6-8-2
4. The rest of the characteristics of the haiku
   apply.

Below are student examples of syllable cinquains:

Rehearse
Without your mask,
Project that naked self
Before costumed eyes--then I shall
Applaud.

                    --Martha Brown
                      12th Grade

I say
I sleep alone--
By God, I lie, because
Only with my dreams of you can
I sleep.

                    --Carolyn Haynes
                      12th Grade

GUITAR

Fondle
The vertical
Strings in the dark, draw from
Them music, coax honey, fulfill
My hunger.

                    --Tom Garvey
                      12th Grade

CONTEMPLATION

Willows
Shake with the breeze
On the cool river bank--
But it is the deep water that
Scares me.

> --Todd Parsons
> 12th Grade

Beware
Women lovers
Caught between their mothers--
Autumn leaves shaking in the wind
May fall.

> --Daloma Armentrout
> 12th Grade

And here are samples of word cinquains:

The child's
Smile sits on wings
Of a laugh not yet spread.
To reach the free flight of youth's mirth,
Laugh young.

> --Elizabeth Plaag
> 12th Grade

Hateful rain
Stabs at my back
Knowing I can never get revenge,
It dances on the ground ahead of me,
Teasing me.

> --Carol Lambert
> 10th Grade

Very young
I read a book,
Not hearing the words until now:
Clouds move: the sun breaks the world into
Light and shade.

> --Carolyn Hudson
> 12th Grade

Exercise 8 - Writing Cinquains: Now try your hand at both word and syllable cinquains. Don't give up until you have at least two good cinquains of each type.

Metaphor and Simile: The Art of Double Vision

The two most natural and most common devices
in poetry for double vision or comparing, that is,
for seeing "connections" between things, are the simile
and the metaphor. A major purpose of both the simile
and the metaphor is to make an abstract concept more
vivid and understandable by comparing it to something
we all "know," something that is <u>physical</u> and <u>concrete</u>.

Since both are comparisons and accomplish the
same purpose, there is a tendency to lump metaphors
and similes together. So, before we start working
with metaphors and similes, let's be sure we have the
same understanding about what they are and how they
differ from each other.

Very simply, a simile expresses a <u>similarity</u>
(notice the root words) between objects <u>directly</u>, by
stating a comparing word such as "like" or "as," e.g.,
"My love is <u>like</u> a red, red rose." A metaphor does
not. A metaphor either states that one thing <u>is</u>
another--"My love is a red, red rose," or implies that
this is the case. For example, in Shakespeare's line
"And summer's lease hath all too short a date", summer
is implied to be a tenant because it has a lease and
the world is implied to be a house because it is for
rent. Brooks and Warren point out that"an essential
difference (between similes and metaphors) is that
metaphors boldly assert an identity: e.g., umbrellas
<u>are</u> blossoms; whereas similes simply point to resem-
blances."[20] Another way of saying it is that similes
request the reader to imagine, side by side, both
the actual object and the image of the object to which
it is being compared. Metaphors, on the other hand,
by establishing that the two objects are identical,
force the reader to superimpose the image of the
actual object on the image of another object. Obviously, the power of both similes and metaphors
derives from the fact that they automatically double
the potential of vision and experience.

Exercise 9 - The Metaphor Game: This game makes an
excellent place to start for the study of metaphors
and similes. Besides, it is a fascinating and fun
game which teaches you a great deal about how you
perceive and are perceived by others. The game asks
you to discover similarities between certain objects

and the people playing the game.   Here is how you play:

Step 1:   Select and write on the board a list of a dozen or so broad categories to use during the game.   Sample categories might be bodies of water, seasons, days of the week, historical periods, types of art, types of music, trees, fabrics, weather types, types of architecture, rooms of a house, pets, wild animals, foods, fruits, junk foods, beverages, etc.

Step 2:   Select a volunteer who will be "it." The role of the volunteer is to ask each class member one metaphorical question, based on the categories the class just selected.   For example, the volunteer might ask questions like: If person X were a room of a house, which room would he/she be?   If person X were a season, which season would he/she be?   If person X were a vegetable. . . ?   And so on.

Step 3:   The volunteer leaves the room while the class selects the person who will be described by answering the metaphorical questions.   It is important that all group members understand who has been selected and that your selection is kept a secret from the volunteer.

Step 4:   After selection of your metaphorical subject ,(whom we'll call Person A) is made, the volunteer returns to the room.   Everyone should be sitting in a circle, with the volunteer inside the circle.   The volunteer goes around the circle, asking each member a metaphorical question as spontaneously as possible, but with as accurate a description of Person A as you can give.   Be careful not to look at Person A as you are answering the question--it will tip off the volunteer as to whom you are describing.

Step 5:   The volunteer may want to write down answers to questions, for his task is to try to put these answers into a composite description and guess who Person A is, who the person is that everyone has been describing through metaphors.   The volunteer has three guesses.

Rules:

1.   With your response to a metaphorical question, you may give a qualification, or the volunteer may ask for one.   For example, if the question were: "If Person A were a body of water, what kind would it be?"   The

response with qualification might be:
"Person A is like a well because he/she's
deep but very self-contained.
2. Only one question is asked each class member.
3. No agreement/disagreement or any comment at
   all should be made regarding a person's
   response to a statement.
4. Several rounds can be played, each time
   selecting a new volunteer and person to be
   described.
5. ENJOY--and listen to how people perceive
   you!

Exercise 10 - Extension of the Metaphor Game: A
natural extension of the metaphor game is to describe
someone you know in a developed and expanded simile
or metaphor. Below is a suggested process:

Step 1. As a lead-up to writing the poem,
you might want to think of the person about whom you
will write in terms of the same categories you used
in the Metaphor Game, or you might prefer to start
fresh. In any case, after you have selected your
metaphor for your person, you might list your specific
bases of comparison. The basis for comparison may be
appearance, behavior, size, shape, color, personality traits, effects, etc., and remember that the
two things being compared should have several qualities in common. In order to identify these common
qualities, you must employ both logic and imagination.

Step 2: Let's look at a student poem written about a classmate. The writer used the metaphor
she responded with in the Metaphor Game, but expanded
it to come up with this:

THE PINK STUDEBAKER

I think, perhaps
There is something to the saying
That people reflect
            the cars they drive.

You are a 1956
        Pink Studebaker,
Pushing your way through
            hundreds of trans-ams and
                    station wagons,
A classic,
        in a milieu of mass produced molds.

```
Pink--is pizzazy, and
              a little questionable--
(Are you ultra-feminine?  Gay?  A PINK Lady???
       Do You Sell Mary Kay Cosmetics?)
```

Other cars will always be envious,
And admire you for your
                    originality.

You are unique,
And you know it.

--Karen King
11th Grade

Step 3: Let's note the bases for similarity used by the writer in developing this metaphor.

1. What is the major point of similarity between the girl being described and a 1956 pink Studebaker? Both are
   classics
   unique, apart from the "mass produced models"
   originals

2. What other details of similarity are noted? Pink is "pizzazy and a little questionable"-- what does this imply about the girl's personality? How does she "feel" about being different? She "pushes her way" through mediocrity, she flaunts it, she knows it.

Step 4: You see? Get very clearly in your mind all the points of similarity you can. Then try your own version, and enjoy sharing your metaphorical descriptions with others!

Here are some other student samples: Following is an example of one student who got beautifully carried away with haiku writing and developing metaphors to describe someone. The result is a metaphor of a person as a haiku. This metaphor stresses the quality of mystery, suggestion, elusiveness, yet lingering fascination over the sense of interrelatedness and understanding between the writer and the person being described. Notice that the structure of the poem is six haikus which come together in an 18 line metaphor.

ELUSIVE HAIKU

Five steps from a jade
Garden you appear wrapped in
Wild leaves and blossoms,
I hear your rhythm--
A thousand locusts droning
Inside; you draw me
Seven steps closer
By curiosity to
Touch this mystery.
So much lies hidden
Within your eyes; they lock with
Mine for an instant--
I capture only
The essence of your beauty:
Echoes of locusts
Vague scents of blossoms,
Before you disappear five steps
Away forever.

> --Karen King
> 12th Grade

Here are some other examples of responses to this
exercise:

BOOK REVIEW

I thought you were easy to read
I liked your style from the very first page
I turned
Your lines were good, but struck me as shallow
so I merely took you as entertainment

You weren't "gripping" and "original"
and I instinctively knew that I <u>would</u> be able to
    put you down

that I could enjoy you
when I wanted . . .

Long ago I finished with you, and was happy.
It was a nice affair without a messy ending

But now I've started remembering
reading new meanings into old lines
sensing plots and themes that I overlooked
In my smugness
And I think I want you back, again.

Are you interested in adding a few chapters?

> --Charlie Moore
> 12th Grade

GLASS BOX

This glass box I keep on my dresser
Reminds me of you--
Sturdy, yet always breakable,
Crystal-clear
But with each facet reflecting back to me
My own face,
And I can only just glimpse
The treasures within,
The pieces of a lifetime's puzzle;
And when I look closer,
Trying to see beyond my own reflection,
The glass fogs over;
I stand back,
Waiting for it to clear,
Content to study the reflection it gives me.

--Juliet Lee
12th Grade

BETH BARBER

She is a pair of brand-new Levis,
That don't quite fit right,
And at first are very uncomfortable.
But the longer you have them,
And the more you wear them,
And after coutless
Washings
They become familiar
And comfortable and even
Necessary.
Your best days are when you are
Wearing them.
Inevitably they will wear out,
Or perhaps become too small,
But you go ahead and keep them
And take them out again and
Try them on, just to
See how they look and remember
The times when you wore them.

--Julianne Parsons
11th Grade

Exercise 11 - Geography of Self: Now let's take the
Metaphor Game and center your attention on you.
Ahh--a little bit harder, right? Possibly, but
you can handle it--and, if you do this exercise pro-
perly, you should learn some fascinating things
about yourself.!

132

Step 1: Imagine you are a country; that is, that your body is a country. Then answer (in any form you wish--written, in your journal, or mentally) the following questions:

1. Take a fantastic voyage, an exploration trip over your body. If you were Lewis and Clark on expedition, what would your journal be like? In your exploration through the new country, what were your discoveries?

2. Take an odyssey into your inner space. How big is the inside of your head? Get a sense of your message network--what is coming in and going out?

3. If your body were a country, where would your rivers be? Population centers? Mountain ranges? Caves? Cliffs?

4. What are the chief products of your country? Natural resources? Material for production? Energy centers? Power plants? Recreation areas and parks?

5. What would you show to tourists?

6. What are the inhabitants of your country like? Who are they? Where do they live? What are they doing? How do they feel about their environment?

7. What are the boundaries of your country?

8. What are the climates and seasons?

9. Where is the capital located? Why?

10. What are your wars and conflicts?

11. Do you own colonies? Who owns a part of you?

12. Where are your frontiers, your unchartered regions?

Step 2: Now concentrate on that part of "Geography" about yourself that you most identified with or thought most interesting, and develop it into a metaphor poem on yourself.

Step 3: You might want to look at these student poems as models:

133

DESERT ISLAND

I am a desert island
Standing steadfast and alone
In a turbulent ocean.
If you long for refuge
From the shark-infested waters,
I gladly welcome you to see it
Beneath my branches of palm.
You will find that I can furnish you
With the basic necessities of life.
Your feet will be sandy,
The mosquitos might bother you,
But you can build a shelter
Of my strong bamboo and green palm tree leaves,
And you can thrive
On nourishing fruits
And coconut milk.

My climate is usually temperate,
But sometimes I am subject to violent storms.
They sweep over me, uprooting trees
And tearing me to pieces,
They are short in duration,
But devastating in strength.
Don't let that keep you away, though.
These storms do not occur often,
And you will learn to endure them
With the passing of time.

It will take time, also
For you to discover all of my secret caves
And grottos.
A few of them house
Dark and dangerous things,
But you will find many
That can provide shelter
From the howling wind
And the pouring rain.

Welcome.
You are always welcome.
But try to remember this cardinal rule
Of desert islands:
During a storm, it is best to seek
The center,
The core of an island
Rather than to tarry at its edges.

--Cathy Read
12th Grade

134

```
                  SIDEWINDER
                        Like a ʹ
                              single
                              sidewinder
                        I cross
                  these
                  sands;
                        I climb
                              the dunes
                              and
                        slide
                  back
            with their
            shifting.
                        Behind
                              I leave
                              a trail
                  of
            scrawled
initials
that
      slowly
                  blur
                        with
                        sand.
                  Cold-
            blooded,
      I
      turn
            my scales
                  against
                              scouring
                              sands;
                        simple-
            minded,
      I
      follow
            a narrow path;
                              and
                              at night
                        the air
            is
      sharp
      and
            heavy
                  with
                        night-
                        blooming
                  cactus
```

135

```
          but
     my blood
   runs
        slowly;
            I

              will
              seek
          the
       cool
     shelter
     beneath
         a rock,
              quiet
                   and
                   dark
           to
       await
     my morning
     thaw.
```

--Juliet Lee
11th Grade

THE DARK GARDEN

Tell me,
What twisted seedlings
Have you planted in their gardens today?
I saw you tilling the fresh, fertile soil
With your spade-tipped tongue.
In your own weed-choked garden
Your paranoia is ample fertilizer
For the pregnant seeds of discontent.
The Deadly Nightshade flourishes;
The Poison Oak and Ivy thrive;
And the black rose grows with deadly thorns,
Until finally your garden is too full,
Too overflowing,
And some of its hideous plants
Must be transplanted to the gardens of others.
If you continue in this brutal scheme,
The sickness and disease will spread
Until even the whitest rose is sullied.

--Cathy Read
12th Grade

Exercise 12 - Extended Metaphors or Similes on
Abstractions: A major purpose of both the simile
and the metaphor is to make an abstract concept more
vivid and understandable by comparing it to something

we all "know," something that is physical and
concrete. At the risk of being redundant, let's
consider again the poem about the girl described as
a 1956 pink Studebaker. We might not know anything
at all about the girl being described; she is an
abstract concept, an "unknown" to us. But we all
have at least a passing knowledge of a 1956 Studebaker,
at least enough to know it would be seen as unique
and different in a group of ordinary trans-ams,
coupes, and station wagons.

Step 1: Below are some professional poems
which define and clarify abstractions by developing
a metaphor or simile. Study these models: (1) by
looking for the bases of comparison on which the poem
is built and (2) by noticing how the language of the
metaphor identifies itself with that of the abstraction.

THE GUITARIST TUNES UP

With that attentive courtesy he bent
Over his instrument;
Not as a lordly conquerer who could
Command both wire and wood,
But as a man with a loved woman might,
Inquiring with delight
What slight essential things she had to say
Before they started, he and she, to play.

--Frances Cornford

RESTAURANTS

Low slung
Modern marvels
Of stone and glass
Sitting on the street
Looking for people to eat
Like architect indians
Scouting the vast uncharted
Frontiers of lunch
Plastic beanery grub mills
Out to kill the appetites
Either by taste or sight
It's like going out to eat
At a hawaiian shirt.[23]

--Mason Williams

THE CENSOR

The Censor sits
Somewhere between
The scenes to be seen
and the television sets
With his scissor purpose poised
Watching the human stuff
That will sizzle through
The magic wires
And light up
Like welding shops
The ho-hum rooms of America
And with a kindergarten
Arts and crafts concept
Of moral responsibility
Snips out
The rough talk
The unpopular opinion
Or anything with teeth
And renders
A pattern of ideas
Full of holes

A doily for your mind.[24]

--Mason Williams

LOVE SONG: I AND THOU

Nothing is plumb, level or square:
    the studs are bowed, the joists
are shaky by nature, no piece fits
    any other piece without a gap
or pinch, and bent nails
    dance all over the surfacing
like maggots. By Christ
    I am no carpenter. I built
the roof for myself, the walls
    for myself, the floors
for myself, and got
    hung up in it myself. I
danced with a purple thumb
    at this house-warming, drunk
with my prime whiskey: rage.
    Oh I spat rage's nails
into the frame-up of my work:
    it held. It settled plumb,
level, solid, square and true
    for that one moment. Then
it screamed and went on through
    skewing as wrong the other way.

138

God damned it. This is hell,
    but I planned it, I sawed it,
I nailed it, and I
    will live in it until it kills me.
I can nail my left palm
    to the left-hand cross-piece but
I can't do everything myself.
    I need a hand to nail the right,
a help, a love, a you, a wife.[25]

                    --Alan Dugan

Step 2: The extended metaphor used to define
an abstraction is a popular technique of modern song-
writers. Consider these examples:

YOU'RE MY HOME

When you look into my eyes
And you see the crazy gypsy in my soul,
It always comes as a surprise
When I feel my withered roots begin to grow.

Well, I never had a place that I could call my
        very own,
But that's alright cuz you're my home.

When you touch my weary head
And you tell me everything will be alright.
You say, "Use my body for your bed and
My love will keep you warm throughout the night."

Well, I'll never be a stranger and I'll never
        be alone,
Whenever we're together, that's my home.

Home to me was the Pennsylvania turnpike,
Indiana early morning dew,
High up in the hills of California
Home is just another word for you.

If I travel all my life and I never get to
        stop and settle down,
As long as I have you by my side,
There's a roof above and four good walls around.

You're my castle, you're my cabin
        and my instant pleasure dome--
I need you in my house 'cause you're my home.
You're my home.[26]

                    --Billy Joel

It's like a dance,
    a demented waltz,
        with all the dancers just a little
            bit mad . . .
Loving, I mean.

Giving in . . . letting go . . .
Taking the chance,
It's like crazy waltz.

Couples in the dance . . .
close . . . apart . . . together . . .
    turning . . . waltzing
Promising more than they can give.

A game of musical chairs,
You play to win . . . But why play so hard?
It's only a waltz.
It's only a time of letting go
    of being someone else for awhile.
But even the waltz ends.

One more time?
Okay
Maybe this one will be different
    From the rest . . .
This one will last . . .
                    maybe[27]

            --Rod McKuen

            I AM A ROCK

A winter's day,
In a deep and dark December.
I am alone gazing from my window
To the streets below.
I'm a freshly fallen silent drop of snow.
            I am a rock
            I am an island.

I build walls
A fortress deep and mighty
That none can penetrate
I have no need of friendship
Friendship causes pain
It's laughter and it's loving I disdain
            I am a rock
            I am an island.

Don't talk of love.
Well, I've heard the word before.
It's sleeping in my memory

I won't disturb the slumber
Of feelings that have died,
If I'd never loved, I never would have cried.
    I am a rock
    I am an island.

I have my books and my poetry to protect me.
I am shielded in my armor.
Hiding in my room,
Safe within my womb, I touch no one
And no one touches me.
    I am a rock
    I am an island.

And a rock feels no pain.
And an island never cries. [28]

    --Simon and Garfunkel

Which do you think are the most effective extended
metaphors? Why? Note: (1) the points of similarity
between the abstraction and the object to which it is
compared, (2) how the language of the metaphor translates the abstraction into concrete, precise images,
(3) the appropriateness, completeness and effective-
ness of the metaphor itself.

   Step 3: Now select an abstraction you want
to work with; probably it would be best to select
one with which you are very familiar. Have you been
jealous lately? Afraid? In love? Guilty? Humili-
ated? Ecstatic? Choose an abstraction you have
personally experienced, then define, clarify and
reveal your feelings about it by developing an
extended metaphor. Use the same process for developing
the metaphor as you used in Exercises 10 and 11.

   Below are some student poems written in
response to this assignment. They might serve as suggestions for structure and approach.

DOUBT

A sudden shadow crept in
Like a black-gloved thief,
Stole from cushion to cushion
And slipped the gleaming smiles
From the faces
Of the pleasant polite;
Slamming the front door in defiance,
He left the room in numb and echoing silence.

They changed the subject hastily,
But still his dark form could be seen,
Lurking behind their eyes.

--Juliet Lee
11th Grade

GUILT

The leprosy began at my mouth
and crawled across my cheeks to my eyes.
It is seated like a tarantula on my face,
and my vision has gone dark.
In this darkness I see disgust and hatred,
and faces mangled by the hand of horror.
All are repelled by a fault not my own.
And I beg them, beseech them
to brush the spider from my brow,
but none will touch me.

--Tom Garvey
12th Grade

GOSSIP

Blazing
Crackling
Shimmering
Greedy tongues
Of gold and amber and ruby-red
Hungrily devouring dry rusty limbs,
Firing them angry red,
Dancing wickedly like demon-shadows
On the impassive brick faces.
Slowly now,
They weary,
Gripping the crumbling coals desperately;
Electric-blue shadows,
The tiny remnants of roaring giants,
Die,
Drifting away in smoky wisps
Curling mournfully up from the heap
Of charred lumps
And dusty ashes.

--Elizabeth Plaag
12th Grade

Exercise 13 - Extended Metaphor/Simile Formula: Below
is another approach or formula for writing an extended
metaphor/simile poem:

By following the steps outlined below, you can
create your own poems centered around a comparison.

Step 1: Focus on an image of some object or
scene which you can imagine clearly. Describe
this image briefly in words which sound well
together.

Step 2: Think about what this image reminds you
of and to what you might compare it. Write
another image which will communicate the comparison you thought of.

Step 3: Show the basis for the comparison you
have made by indicating some way(s) in which the
first and second images are alike.

Step 4: Decide how you feel about the object
or scene you are writing about. Indicate your
own feelings about it in a line or two.

Triple Vision: Perceiving Relationships Through Symbol

Another natural centering process is through
symbol. If double vision is comparing or seeing
connections between things by metaphor or simile, the
symbol is a natural step beyond--into triple vision.
What (exactly) is a symbol and how does it differ
from a metaphor?

Broadly defined, a symbol is a sign that does
not exist for its own, but instead points to a meaning
beyond itself. For example, words, numbers, the
plus/minus signs, notes and marks on a musical staff,
traffic signs, a striped pole outside a barber shop
are all symbols. Its significance resides in the
meaning it carries beyond itself.

A literary symbol, which is the kind we are
concerned with here, is a thing (an event, person,
object, quality, or a relationship) that functions
simultaneously in two ways: (a) as itself, and (b) as
a sign of something outside itself. There are two
kinds of literary symbols: (1) Conventional (or
traditional) symbols, which are objects that, by
customary association and general assignment, have a
certain significance and meaning. They are common,
and recurrent in both art and life, having the same
meaning in universal experience. (2) Nonce (or

143

personal) symbols, which are symbols that the writer
himself invents "for the nonce," which means "for the
present." Nonce is derived from the Angle-Saxon anon,
meaning now. So, nonce symbols are symbols that
accumulate meaning largely in our own personal experiences and generally for a particular purpose or occa-
sion known only to the writer.

Exercise 14 - Determining Conventional and Nonce
Symbols Through Fantasy: To clarify distinctions in
your own mind between conventional and nonce symbols, let's go on a fantasy trip. It will be a
guided fantasy, and it is important that the following
conditions are met: (1) get into your own space
where you will be comfortable and undisturbed by
others; (2) your eyes should be closed, and the
lights turned off; (3) there should be total silence,
except for the voice of the person guiding the
fantasy; (4) free your mind and follow the instructions of the guide, without forcing or censoring
the direction of your thoughts.

        Below are the instructions for the fantasy·
trip:

        Imagine that you are walking through a
    forest in the afternoon. What does the forest
    look like? Imagine it in your mind. As you
    are walking, you suddenly meet a bear. Ima-
    gine what you do. Imagine now that the bear
    has disappeared and you are continuing to
    walk through the forest. You find a key.
    Imagine what it looks like and what you do with
    it. You continue on and come to some kind of
    water. Imagine what it looks like. Not far
    away you see a cup; you go over and pick it
    up. Then what do you do with it? You continue
    walking and now the forest ends and before you
    is a long stretch--as far as the eye can see--of
    flat land without any trees. Imagine what this
    flat land looks like. Sitting in the midst of
    this flat land is a building or house of some
    kind. Imagine what it looks like. If you
    want to enter this building, you may. If you
    decide to enter, imagine that you go inside and
    wander through the rooms. If there is a door
    or a window in the building, walk over to it
    and look outside. What do you see?[30]

        After the fantasy trip, your guide through
the fantasy should give you the following information

144

about the meaning of the symbols in the fantasy, which most psychologists would agree to be universal and traditional meanings.[31]

Symbols	What They Represent
forest	your life (Is it pleasant? Can you see where you're going, or is it so cluttered that you feel you're in a maze? etc.)
bear	a problem (How did you deal with it? Run away? Meet it head on? etc.)
key	yourself (How do you imagine yourself? Are you bright shiny? What do you do with the key? Cherish it? Throw it away?)
cup	your attitude toward love or other strong emotions (Do you use the cup? Throw it away? etc.)
flat land	old age (Is it a meadow? A desert?)
building	death (If you're willing to enter the building, you can face the fact of death.)
view from the window	your vision of life after death (If the building had no windows, you do not admit or believe in life after death.)

What did you discover about yourself as a result of this experience? Do you buy the interpretation of the symbols as Jung translates them? Why? Why not? It is most interesting at this point to compare and discuss how your fantasy was similar to or different from others in regard to how your fantasy employed these symbols. One of the most important aspects of this exercise is the discovery that everyone's mind almost automatically produces and translates symbols: that, in fact, symbol-making is a natural centering activity.

Exercise 15 - Free Association with Symbols: Now let's apply the principles of free association to symbols.

145

Step 1: Below is a list of traditional symbols. Select five words and for each, make two columns, one for associations you feel would be traditional, and one for associations you feel are your personal individual associations with that word.

Winter	Sun	Star
Spring	Rain	Wine
Serpent	Mountain	White
Moon	Sea	Black

Step 2: After you have listed traditional and nonce associations for five words, it would be helpful to compare your associations with others. Are some of the associations you thought were personal mentioned by others? Are some associations you thought would be traditional only your own, personal associations?

Step 3: Now compare your associations with the following list of traditional symbols that appear frequently in both English and American poetry. This list of symbols is obviously incomplete, but it contains many of the most commonly used traditional symbols.

Symbols	What They Represent
winter, (the color white, snow, ice cold)	old age, death, solitude
spring (the color green, new growth)	rebirth, childhood, hopefulness
summer (flowers, the color gold, sun, warmth)	youth, ease, luxury
fall (harvests, full moon, the color yellow)	middle age, fullness, loss of youth
bride (the color white, a maiden, roses)	the Church, purity, innocence
groom	Christ
serpent (a sinuous or twisted shape, a worm)	evil, Satan

146

cross (wood, nails, thorns	the crucifixion
wine (grapes)	the sacrament, the resurrection, new life or strength
sun (fire, heat, the color red)	passion, strong feeling, love
stars (light, brightness)	faith, eternity, the unattainable
rain	loss, death, tears
sea (tides, sand)	the passage of time
voyages (rivers, paths, roads)	the journey through life
heights (mountains, hills)	the difficult to attain, heaven
house (building, monument, stone)	death, the grave
music (bird call, a song, pan-pipes)	enchantment, oblivion
moon (the colors white and silver)	blue and black, night, germination and the original void
shapes (circle and crescent)	containers--cup, cauldron, boat, coffin
triangle	in 3-dimensional, cone or pillar
animals (rabbit and snake)	fertility and transformation
(crescent-horned animals)	visual kinship
(water animals)	fish, crab
(nocturnal)	owl
(birds)	doves, peacocks, swans, swallow, bluebird, goose
elements:	
blood	vitality
water	mutability
fire	illumination
stone	permanence
plants	mistletoe, lily, palm

egg (shape of the orbit of the moon)	is the one that unites all her aspects; mother and source of fertility to earth; origin and end of all effort; heart center
circle	universal symbol of wholeness, without beginning and end; corresponds to the os or circular opening to the womb from which we all enter life; repetitive cycles
variations	point, origin and infinity; hole, gateway to another consciousness; pole (May Pole) marks the mystic point of center; cross, also represents center where two lines intersect in centerpoint
number two	reflection, echo, integration and duality, the double
spiral	breath of the Spirit power, the dance; contracting and expanding; ecstasy
crescent	aspect of change or transformation in the world; linked to water as representation of the boat and the chalice; sickle of death and cup of life
weaving	creation of the world
spiders	in their webs, weavers like the Fates; building, tearing down, rebuilding
veil	said to cover the mystery of the world; cloth is the product of the moon's work
musical instruments made in lunar forms	combinations of masculine and feminine shapes, representing androgyny, unity, and sexuality; blending of the spirit

148

key	opener of the door to the world; signifies the stage; after great difficulty, just prior to the discovery of a great treasure
butterfly	alternation between appearance and disappearance
shells	legs and pubic triangle of the Great Mother (shape of the toad)
bees	complexity; queen of the hive; bee-souls returning to the source
tree	life at the center of the world
rose	love and perfection
lotus	mystic center inside many layers; this and rose are forms of the mandala
lily	purity and light
flowering plants with thorns	inseparable cycle of life and death
ruler	decision-maker, state of affairs
musician	singer, dancer of life
poet	teller of tales, writer, creator of drama
artist	visionary, conveyor of reality and dreams
philosopher	scholar, intellectual
scientist	discover
explorer	guide to new age
physician	healer
theologian	spiritual advisor, Christian leader
political activist	social changer

The following poems each employ traditional symbols in much the same way as those used in the fantasy trip. It should be helpful for you to see how they are used in poetry:

Poems using forest or trees as symbols for life:

> "Stopping by Woods on a Snowy Evening"--
> Robert Frost
> "Road Not Taken"--Robert Frost
> "Spring and Fall"--Gerard Manley Hopkins

Poems using a house as a symbol for death:

> "The House on a Hill"--E. A. Robinson
> "The Deserted House"--Alfred, Lord Tennyson

Poems using the journey as a symbol of life experience:

> "The Wayfarer"--Stephen Crane
> "The Long Hill"--Sara Teasdale
> "The Dump"--Donald Hall

O.K., if you feel you understand the distinction between traditional and nonce symbols, let's consider more complex and more subtle aspects of using symbols in writing. Here are some important points to keep in mind:

1. The purpose of the use of symbols is to allow the poet to communicate two levels of meaning simultaneously: (a) the literal level, at which the symbolic objects represent real objects; and (b) the symbolic level, at which the symbolic objects represent more than mere objects, usually something of far greater significance than the symbol itself.

2. The "something" that the symbol stands for is usually unstated, so several interpretations of what a single symbol represents may be possible.

3. Associations are a crucial part of working with symbols. In using traditional symbols, there are usually logical connections between the symbol and what it represents. For example, spring, because it begins the yearly cycle of planting, marks a time of renewal in nature, and so spring logically has become a traditional symbol of hope, youth, and rebirth. On the other hand, associations and connections with nonce

150

symbols are more difficult. So, the writer must be very careful to include these personal associations and connections within your poem so the symbols do not seem arbitrary.

4. Distinctions between the metaphor and symbol are often vague. Perhaps the best discussion of this distinction is made in Brooks and Warren, Understanding Poetry, in which the following points of difference are made.[33]

   (1) In symbolic poetry, the thing for which a symbol stands is often left unstated; both are always stated in a metaphor.

   (2) A metaphor cannot be taken literally; a symbolic poem functions simultaneously on both the literal and symbolic level.

   (3) In a symbol poem you have a replacement of one thing by another thing; in a metaphor, you have a comparison of two things.

For example, consider this poem by William Blake:

THE SICK ROSE

O Rose, thou art sick.
The invisible worm
That flies in the night
In the howling storm
Has found out thy bed
Of crimson joy,
And his dark secret love
Does thy life destroy.[3]

If this poem were an extended metaphor, Blake would have stated what the rose, and what the worm represented, such as "Evil is a worm that destroys beauty"; instead, the poem functions literally; a worm can reside in a rose, invisible to the eye, and destroy its life.

Exercise 16 - Using Music to Distinguish Between Metaphor and Symbol: Below is a list of popular songs. Listen carefully to the lyrics (it would be helpful to look at the lyrics), and determine which are the purest, clearest examples of the use of symbol:

   "Woodstock" by Joni Mitchell
   "Hotel California" by The Eagles
   "Song Bird" by Barbra Streisand

"Windflower" by Seals and Croft
"Diamonds and Rust" by Joan Baez
"Both Sides Now" by Joni Mitchell
"Stairway to Heaven" by Led Zeppelin
"Tapestry" by Carole King

As a structure for your consideration, apply the three distinctions between metaphor and symbol we discussed earlier.

Exercise 17 - A Personal Symbol:

 Step 1: Bring to class an object that is a personal symbol for you or some part of you--an experience, a time in your life, a quality you love or hate, a relationship. Share that object, that part of yourself, that personal symbol, with the class. Then use that object as the basis for a symbol poem.

 Step 2: As preparation for the actual writing of the poem, fill in this chart concerning the object you've shared with the class as your personal symbol:

Your Personal Symbol	Thing or Quality It Represents	Points of Similarity
Secondary Symbols	Secondary Qualities	

 Step 3: If you can fill out that chart, you are probably ready to write your symbol poem. If you can't, you need to think through the symbol more thoroughly.

 Perhaps studying the following symbol poems would help:

ROSES

I gave you a rose
Blood red
And perfect
A single small perfect rose.

152

Someday,
I'll give you
A bouquet
Of roses.
Some blood red ones, yes.
But also
Some onyx black ones,
Even more rare and perfect.
Black and red roses
On long thorny stems.
They won't be on a
Cushion of green leaves
Of fern.
Just the bold flowers
You must provide the green
To soften their starkness.

--Julianne Parsons
11th Grade

THE SLUG

I won't step on you yet,
Even though
I despise
You, the lump
Of pale dough
That slouches across
My garden,
Leaving a trail
Of slick slime behind.
And when I put my face close
To the deep perfumed velvet
Of a rose
And again find
You, hidden there,
Crawling along the curving red lips,
Crusting them with slime,
And I drop it
From frozen fingers
And you wiggle free:
Still I won't step on you;
I'll merely move away.
But one day
When I can stand the feel
Of slime
On my skin
I will raise my foot
And hold it squarely above you
And bear down
And grind;

For I am a slug-crusher,
And I will keep my garden free
Of creatures like you.

--Juliet Lee
11th Grade

SHELL AND SAND (CONCEIT)

Shell likes being noticed,
Glinting on all that white,
Rippling in its beauty.
Hold it to any ear
And let it whisper its own praises,
Praises that are nothing but empty wind.
Drop it from any hand
And let it fall crashing
Back to white where it will not
Rest, but only continue whispering
While the sand slides in
And begins to fill it,
Cutting off any winds.
A silent burial,
Shell and sand.

--Cathy Cain
10th Grade

STRENGTH

There is a large grey stone
On the edge of a small forest
It sits in the shade and thinks,
While birds come and sing on it,
And squirrels come and crack their
Nuts on it.
A small badger lives underneath it
And only comes out when some other
Animal comes too close.
When rabbits come to life in its
Shade it never complains but
Never encourages.
It just sits and smiles
And listens to the songs
Of the birds and watches the
Scampering of the small animals.
A small red fox lives in the woods
And comes by every now and then
Frightening the other animals away.
But it never frightened the stone.
It was too big and too strong,
That's why the animals like it.

It gave them what they needed
And they never had to give it anything
In return.
It was too strong.

--Julianne Parsons
11th Grade

Step 4: Try filling in the chart above to break down the poet's use of symbol in at least one of these poems. That should clarify whatever problems you might be having.

Step 5: Now write your symbol poem. Good luck--and enjoy!

Exercise 18 - Working with Traditional Symbols: Traditional symbols surround us in our daily lives--they abound in advertising and cliches (unfortunately), and they are the heart pumping life blood (ah-ha! a symbol! or was it a metaphor?) into proverbs and epigrams.

Step 1: Consider the well-known proverbs below:

Every cloud has a silvery lining . . .

A rolling stone gathers no moss . . .

Every rose has its thorn . . .

The squeaky wheel gets the grease . . .

Where there's smoke, there's fire . . .

Any port in a storm . . .

Each man forges his own fetters . . .

You can't make a silk purse out of a sow's ear . . .

Empty barrels make the most noise . . .

Because symbols are common and natural means of expression, too often they are overlooked or are only vaguely understood.

Step 2: Take each of the proverbs above and explain precisely and specifically what the symbols in each proverb stand for.

Step 3: Now study the professional poems below which are built around traditional symbols:

155

"Fern Hill" by Dylan Thomas
"A White Rose" by O'Reilly
"Fire and Ice" by Robert Frost
"Curiosity" by Alastair Reid
"Snake" by D. H. Lawrence

CURIOSITY

may have killed the cat; more likely
the cat was just unlucky, or else curious
to see what death was like, having no cause
to go on licking paws, or fathering
litter on litter of kittens, predictably.

    Nevertheless, to be curious
is dangerous enough. To distrust
what is always said, what seems
to ask odd questions, interfere in dreams,
leave home, smell rats, have hunches
does not endear him to those doggy circles
where well-smelt baskets, suitable wives, good
      lunches
are the order of incurious heads and tails.

    Face it   Curiosity
will not cause him to die--
only lack of it will.
Never to want to see
the other side of the hill,
or that improbable country
where living is an idyll
(although a probable hell)
would kill us all.
Only the curious
have, if they live, a tale
worth telling at all.

    Dogs say he loves too much, is irresponsible,
is changeable, marries too many wives,
deserts his children, chills all dinner tables
with tales of his nine lives.
Well, he is lucky. Let him be
nine-lived and contradictory,
curious enough to change, prepared to pay
the cat price, which is to die
and die again and again.
each time with no less pain.
A cat minority of one
is all that can be counted on
to tell the truth. And what he has to tell
on each return from hell

is this: That dying is what the living do,
and that dead dogs are those who do not know
that hell is where, to live, they have to go.[35]

                    --Alastair Reid

        Do you feel at all like a Peter Bell now?
Hopfully not--hopefully, all this practice in perceiving relationships, in becoming attune to your own
natural associations, in seeing your world and your
experiences through similes, metaphors and symbols,
you've doubled and tripled your vision! Perhaps you
are becoming more and more centered!

FOOTNOTES: CHAPTER V

[1]Marilyn Ferguson, The Aquarian Conspiracy (Los Angeles: J. P. Tarcher, Inc., 1980), 304-305.

[2]Richard Cattell, "The Structure of Intelligence in Relation to the Nature-Nuture Controversy," in W. R. Cancro (ed.), Intelligence, Genetic and Environmental Influences (New York: Green and Stratton, 1971); Beverly Galyean, "The Brain, Intelligence and Education: Implications for Gifted Programs," Position Paper presented to the State Department of Education, Division of Gifted and Talented (January, 1981), 5.

[3]Robert Hershon, "On Horror," 31 New American Poets, Ron Schreiber, ed. (New York: Hill and Wang, 1969), 94-95.

[4]Robert Frost as quoted at Breadloaf Writers Conference, Middlebury, Vermont, Summer, 1967.

[5]Archibald MacLeish, "Ars Poetica," Poetry Is For People, Martha McDonough and William C. Doster, eds (Boston: Allyn and Bacon, Inc., 1965), 2.

[6]Carl Sandburg, "Poetry Is . . . ," Complete Poems (New York: Harcourt Brace and World, Inc., 1950), 317-319.

[7]Lawrence Ferlinghetti, "Constantly Risking Absurdity," Poetry Is For People, 220-21.

[8]Lou Lipsitz, "Skinny Poem," The Young American Poets, Paul Carroll, ed. (New York: Follett Publishing Co., 1968), 246-47.

[9]Phillip Hey, "The Poem That Tries To Be A Tree," The Young American Poets, 195-96.

[10]Ken MacCrorie, Writing To Be Read (New York: Hayden Book Co., Inc., 1978), 144.

[11]Ezra Pound, quoted in MacCrorie (1978), 144.

[12]Marianne Moore, quoted in MacCrorie (1978), 147.

CHAPTER VI

PATTERN-MAKÍNG:
BRIDGING OBJECTIVE EXPERIENCE WITH IMAGINATION

> One writes out of one thing only--one's
> own experience. Everything depends on how
> relentlessly one forces from this experience
> the last drop, sweet or bitter, it can pos-
> sibly give. This is the only real concern
> of the artist, to recreate out of the
> disorder of life that order which is art.[1]

> --James Baldwin

To recreate order out of the disorder of
life is one goal of centering. By centering ourselves, by finding that quiet, still, unwobbling,
stable, creative center within ourselves, we balance
the inner and outer worlds of experience. Our inner
and outer lives present us with a dichotomy: the
world of the familiar, the "real", the "physical",
the realm of fact and senses; the world of the
intangible, the world of imagination, emotion, fantasy, dream, and memory; the world of right brain,
subjective knowing. To be centered, we must be aware
of, consciously in tune with, both--and comfortable
with both. Then we must be able to adjust each world
to the other and to our vision and perspective of
experiences. Well, easy enough to say--right? But
very difficult to do. But remember--nobody promised
you that writing was easy. . . . But let's go on--all
the really fun challenges are ahead of us.

In Chapters II and III we dealt with simply
becoming more conscious of our physical senses,
tuning in to our world of experience, the objective
world outside our skin. In short, we dealt with
developing our sense of sense, of the "here and now."
Although this process is necessary, it is not the
main point. It is fine to learn to love the actual and
sensual, to accumulate details in every corner of the
attic of the mind, to become fascinated with the
"is-ness" and the "what-ness", but soon at least two
problems develop: (1) You have no file-clerk, and
the walls bulge and the rafters sag with the chaotic
confusion of all this inaccessible detail. (2) Writing,
creative writing that is, is not a catalog of these

facts of experience; that is journalism. (3) Centering is a balance, not a lopsidedness.

So we must learn to walk the line, more taut than any tightrope, between this yearning for concreteness, for "truth" that can be felt between the fingers and counted--and the imagination, the insight, that gives meaning to those facts and details of experience. In short, we yearn for a centering of left and right hemispheres. Without this imaginative balancing, the facts are only facts, and the writer cops out on going the next step and discovering what the experience means. Do not misunderstand me: This is not to say that the writer must interpret this experience for the reader, but it is to say that until we know the meaning of that experience for ourselves, we can not present the experience imaginatively, insightfully, or intuitively to anyone else. The following exercises will help you deal with your own experiences and senses more insightfully through imagination, and will give you experience in centering these inner and outer worlds.

On Isolating Fabulous Realities

All right--given the fact that our lives are an overwhelming accumulation of sensory fact and experience, one of our first tasks is to isolate an experience from experience in general: to use our insight, our imagination, to recognize a unit in life which has some explicit meaning or emotional impact. To do this, we must constantly expect those moments which Thoreau describes as "fabulous":

> Shams and delusions are esteemed for soundest truth, while reality is fabulous. If men would steadily observe realities only, and not allow themselves to be deluded, life, to compare it with such things as we know, would be like a fairy tale and the Arabian Night's Entertainments.[2]
>
> --Henry Thoreau

The following is an excerpt from Ken MacCrorie's Writing To Be Read and offers an excellent discussion of "fabulous realities":[3]

> Most of us go through each day looking for what we saw yesterday and we find it, to our half-realized disappointment. All our

todays become dull yesterdays. But the man
who daily expects to encounter fabulous
realities runs smack into them again and
again. He keeps his mind open for his eyes.

Asked to expect surprise, a number of students
explored their nearby worlds for fabulous realities.
Here are some they found:

1. A Band-Aid on a small tree.

2. A roll of toilet paper on the lawn of the
   university maintenance building.

3. A pregnant woman carrying a globe of the
   world in front of her up a steep sidewalk
   in the city.

4. On Sunday morning a boy walking down the main
   street wrapped in a pink blanket with a New
   Era potato chip can over his head.

5. Sign in a downtown arcade: "Four Barbers.
   No Waiting." And then below: "Television
   While You Wait."

6. Under a parked car, a lollipop lying in oil.

7. On the envelope, the postage meter message:
   "Fly the fastest route to the Orient via
   Northwest Orient Airlines." Next to it, the
   Detroit Post Office's cancelling message:
   "Discover a new world, see the U.S.A."

8. "Help the poor kitty, Honey!" screamed the
   girl at the curb. Her boy friend stopped
   and looked down at the grey and white
   mangled, lifeless animal with the label on
   it reading "Made at Sears Toyland."

9. At a busy intersection I saw a white-haired
   woman scooping up spilled dry oatmeal from
   the street after the bottom of her grocery
   bag had burst. She was explaining to a
   honking motorist that she didn't want to waste
   the oatmeal--she was going to take it home
   to her ducks.

10. Last fall a blind man with a white-striped
    cane passed a kindergarten class searching
    for leaves. A boy walked all the way back
    to school with his eyes closed.

Each of these statements surprises. It is not fairly
surprising, but absolutely surprising, because it is

unique. A robin sitting in the April snow in Illinois
or Massachusetts would not qualify as a fabulous
reality. Often these states experience a short snow
after robins have arrived. Tension is necessary--two
things which do not belong together touch in some
way. And their touching creates waves of further
suggestion that are not stated. The boy is not walking
down a street wrapped in a pink blanket on Monday,
but down the main street on Sunday, when others are
dressed in Sunday-go-to-church clothes. Going to
the Orient and discovering a new world in the United
States are notions that create more than a simple
contradiction together. They make the reader think
of how little he knows of China or how persons quick
to give him advice like "Go west, young man" are
telling only half the possibilities of life. Written
in concise form, these fabulous realities are complete
in themselves and at the same time pregnant, like the
woman walking up the hill, with worlds of thought yet
to be explored--doors, beginnings, for further
writing. They may be suggestive on several levels.
The person who reported the woman explaining about .
her ducks to the honking motorists might note that
ducks honk, too.

Exercise 1 - Finding Fabulous Realities:

    Step 1: O.K., now you try it! In your
journal for the next week, record all of the "fabulous realities" you can find. Remember to look for
what is unusual, not your "run-of-the-mill" reality,
but that which surprises, which has tension, that
which suggests several levels of meanings.

    Step 2: Once you have collected some fabu-
lous realities, you need to work on stating them in
such a way that you build up the surprises, and that
you re-create its reality as strongly for the reader
as you felt it.

    A writer must remain sensitive to one's own
anticipations as well as the reader's, if he/she is
to perceive the tension between a fact and its context which creates surprise. That is a matter of
seeing truth and writing it honestly.

    The writer who tries for truth will not
pretend to see fabulous realities constantly; for
if everything is surprising, nothing is surprising.

    Step 3: Now that you've stated your fabulous
realities well, see if one of them offers itself to be

developed into a longer piece, either a poem or a short story. Here are some student examples of an expanded fabulous reality:

My cat was a Ballerina:
 pirouetted after dust motes,
 pirouetted after furred tails,
 pirouetted after spinning leaves,
 and, after the car,
   one last pirouette.

     --Charlie Moore
     12th Grade

We mistook those graves
 for picnic tables, and ate
dead cows on dead men.

     --Kevin Kuykendall
     12th Grade

RED TIGHTS

Red tights--
She wore
Red tights
To church
On a shadow-cast Sunday
And high above
In his pulpit
The preacher
Saw red;
And he thought
Of the red fires
Of Hell
As she crossed her legs;
And he thought
Of the red thunder
Of righteousness
As she swung her ankle;
And he thought
Of the red wrath
Of God
As she flexed her smooth calf;
And he thought
Of that juicy red apple
That first tempted Man--
But above his dark robes
His face was deep red
As he thought
Of those red, red tights.

     --Juliet Lee
     11th Grade

Here is a professional poem which began by recognizing a fabulous reality:

A BOY ON LOOKING AT BIG DAVID

I'm touching his toe.
I know I'll be brave after this.
His toenail wide as my hand,
I have to stand tall to reach it.

The big loose hand with the rock in it
by his thigh
is high above my head. The vein
from wrist to thumb, a blue strain in the marble.

As if it had natural anatomy all its own
inside it.
Somebody skinned off the top stone
and there He stands.

I'd like to climb up there on that slippery hip,
shinny up to the shoulder
the other side of that thumping Neck,
and lie in the ledge on the collar-bone,
by the sling.
In that cool place
I'd stare-worship that big, full-lipped,
frown-browned, far-eyed, I-dare-you-Face.

I'd like to live on that David for a while,
get to know
how to be immortal like Him.
But I can only reach his Toe--

broad, poking only the edge of the stand.
So cool . . .
Maybe, marble Him,
he likes the warm of my hand?[4]

                                        --May Swenson

You see? This kind of expectation, this way to seeing reality as a fascination and mystery, this type of discovery, is made only through imagination, insight. It is not a gimmick; it is not just an exercise. It is the way good writers experience the moments in their lives--by recognizing and isolating those special ones--and centering them.

Memory: The Abstract World of Experience

Another world of experience, of fabulous realities, can be reached through our memory. Think of it--all of experience is only a memory, except for

this present moment--and oops! It is a memory now as
it slides away into the past as we think these
thoughts. So if you do not use your memory as a
resource for writing, you are eliminating most of
your material. However, writing about a memory has
its difficulties:

> But don't expect to write well about the
> love affair that you are in the midst of,
> or have just mailed a letter to break off.
> One principal figure in that situation you
> can't see. At least one. Probably two. You
> are "involved." You don't surround it.
> You suffer or you triumph; you do not compre-
> hend.
>
> Later, all those feelings will become
> your knowledge. They will be of your know-
> ledge and wisdom when they no longer possess
> you. Your subject must be something you pos-
> sess and can move all the way around. The
> former feelings that come together in your
> subject may include the most glorious or
> devastating that you ever had. And you will
> re-experience them. But you most emotionally
> enclose and dominate them. [5]

--Sidney Cox

The process of remembering is an abstract
act of the imagination, and writers do it because it
is necessary. We move into the past because the past
is a part of us; remembering moves us closer to our
origins, to ourselves, to the children we were and to
the children around us today. We go back because the
past defines and shapes the future and because in
writing through those years, we gain a second life,
this time a more conscious one.

All writers take this journey. May Swenson
went back to childhood like this:

THE CENTAUR

> The summer that I was ten--
> can it be there was only one
> summer that I was ten? It must
>
> have been a long one then--
> each day I'd go out to choose
> a fresh horse from my stable

which was a willow grove
down by the old canal.
I'd go on my two bare feet.

But when, with my brother's jack-knife,
I had cut me a long limber horse
with a good thick knob for a head,

and peeled him slick and clean
except a few leaves for the tail,
and cinched my brother's belt

around his head for a rein,
I'd straddle and canter him fast
up the grass bank to the path,

trot along in the lovely dust
that talcumed over his hoofs,
hiding my toes, and turning

his feet into swift half-moons.
The willow knob with the strap
jouncing between my thighs

was the pommel and yet the poll
of my nickering pony's head.
My head and my neck were mine,

yet they were shaped like a horse.
My hair flopped to the side
like the mane of a horse in the wind.

My forelock swung in my eyes,
my neck arched and I snorted.
I shied and skittered and reared,

stopped and raised my knees,
pawed at the ground and quivered.
My teeth bared as we wheeled

and swished through the dust again.
I was the horse and the rider,
and the leather I slapped to his rump

spanked my own behind.
At a walk we drew up to the porch,
my thighs hugging his ribs.

Dismounting, I smoothed my skirt
and entered the dusky hall.
My feet on the clean linoleum
left ghostly toes in the hall.

"Where have you been?" said my mother.
"Been riding," I said from the sink,
and filled me a glass of water.

"What's that in your pocket?" she said.
"Just my knife." It weighted my pocket
and stretched my dress awry.

"Go tie back your hair," said my mother,
and "Why is your mouth all green?"
"Rob Roy, he pulled some clover
as we crossed the field," I told her. [6]

Exercise 2 - Recording a Memory: Yes, you guessed it!
Now it is time for you to try it. Please follow this
process: Choose from your childhood a moment you
can't forget. Write it down, and concentrate on
putting the reader there by re-creating as many "real"
sense details as you can. Don't worry at this point
about form or word choice; just try to record and to
re-experience the experience. Get the facts of the
experience down. We'll come back to this memory later.

Exercise 3 - Undeceiving Yourself: Now comes the hard
part in dealing with memory: Memory has the curious
capacity to change the facts of the past experience
to suit our ego, and sometimes it is hard to know
what really happened. Given the same event, two
people might remember the facts quite differently.
We all admit that--so granting that the idea of sincerity and honesty is tricky, it must also be admitted
that it is a very valuable and necessary idea. If
we think further about it, it has everything to do
with the reasons to write at all--and is crucial to
writing well! Peter Elbow, in an excellent book,
Uptaught, observes:

> I warn against defining sincerity, as telling
> true things about oneself. It is more accurate
> to define it functionally as the sound of a
> writer's voice or self on paper . . . a general
> sound of authenticity in words. The point is
> that self-revelation is an easy route in our
> culture and therefore can be used as an eva-
> sion; it can be functionally insincere even if
> substantially true and intimate. To be precise,
> sincerity is the elimination of "noise" or
> static--the ability or courage not to hide the
> real message. [7]

The static is the distance between what
the words say and what sense lies behind them. The
person with a pose of sincerity fixes us with his
eyes, saying, "I'm going to be wholly honest with
you. I am a bastard. I cheat on my wife and I fink

on my business partner. I hate my father because he gave me a car. I hit a blind man once when nobody was looking." The real message: "Love me, I'm so honest."

The distance between the meaning (the apparently stated) and the expressed (the really implied) is the sickness.[8]

We all know that many feelings are falsely expressed. We have all heard people say on the telephone, "I'm so sorry I can't come!" when we knew they could but didn't want to come. And we have done the same thing. We have grown up on the false laughter of television, the false enthusiasm of advertising, the commercial jollity and condolences of greeting cards, the lying assertions of politicans and the double standards of parents and educators. If some falsity had not entered our writing, we'd be of aluminum.

There are a thousand ways to be false and dishonest. We do it with handshakes; we do it with grunts and gestures and facial expressions; and we do it with outright lies. But at least we know they are lies if we give it a moment's thought. When we fool ourselves (which we do frequently), we are in real trouble. We are off center.

HERE COMES THE RUB: Functional sincerity that Elbow talks about comes from self-knowledge that is the result of self-exploration. It is not easy. Most deceptive writing occurs unconsciously because we do not know ourselves well enough to know what we meant to say! Honesty in writing requires first that you are honest with yourself; it requires self-examination and hard thinking and hard looking at yourself. It is worth it. Socrates observed that the unexamined life is not worth living. This is especially true of a writer's life.

As persons who want to be centered, and as writers, just trying to be very conscious will help tremendously. So will developing a habit of testing what you write, as well as what you read and hear, for honesty.

Ken MacCrorie suggests the following as characteristics of ways we unconsciously deceive ourselves in writing:

We have

1) not written about what really motivated us to put pen to paper; or
2) not spoken truly when we thought we were being faithful to the world we experienced; or
3) told only a small part of the truth; or
4) forgotten to tell the reader the facts that make convincing what we insist the reader must be overwhelmed by; or
5) grandly asked questions that everyone knows the answer to; or
6) apologized for not being an expert on what we write page or pages about; or
7) used awkward and phony language that does not belong to him, or
8) used six words where the reader only needed two.[9]

O.K.--if we accept the premise that a major requirement is to be honest and truthful, how can we go about learning to <u>undeceive ourselves</u>? One way is through writing out your memories. For example, look at the two poems below.[10] Both are memory poems and deal with the same subject. One poem generalizes the knowledge instead of putting the reader through the experience in a factual, honest way. One poem speaks only to the poet and yet expects the reader to be fascinated by an experience not recorded (an act called private writing). Read and compare these two poems. Which deals with the memory honesty by re-creating the experience? Which is dishonest? Which <u>talks about the experience</u>? Which seems most controlled by the poet's ego?

SORROW: MY TRUE STORY

Now, I want to tell you people
My true story and it's sad.
I will shout it from the hilltops
How I really had it bad.

How I cried each night just for him,
How I missed him when he left.
I believed the lies he told me,
I might as well have been deaf.

Then his heart grew tired and restless
And he soon stopped wanting me.
He would flirt behind my back
And he thought I didn't see.

Now, I know he was unfaithful,
But my hurt just wouldn't show

For I loved him, too much even
to ever let him go.

I wonder as I look back if
I did right, or was I wrong?
To let him think he deceived me
When I knew it all along.

He finally asked for his freedom
So I had to let him go
Now my friends say to forget him;
Now my smile is just a show.

They don't even know that when I hear his name
All the memories creep inside
Then my heart is filled with
Sadness and the tears are hard to hide.

I'm sure you recognize my story
For it happened to you too.
That's why I'm shouting from this hilltop
How did it end with YOU???

MISSING

You belong here with me
        on a night like this.
You are a part of it.
Your leaky old car
        parked outside the house,
        the dry smell of your hair
        the man-sweet smell
        of your freshly washed shirt.
But tonight
        all that are left
        are oil stains
        in a drip-drop pattern
        by the curb.

And they get dimmer
        with every rain.

    The person who speaks in "Sorrow" cried, she
missed her boyfriend, he told her lies, he stopped
seeing her, he flirted behind her back. This is a
pattern of experience that almost every girl has
known, yet the writer tells not one convincing
detail--what was the boy like? How could he hold
her when he treated her so badly? Were they blatant
or devious lies? Finally, she says she let him go.
Was she in a position to let him go? He had already
gone. . . . In the fifth stanza, she asks what
might be a penetrating question, but does she really
wonder? She accuses him of deceiving her then admits

deceiving him. If she had faced this question
squarely and probed the reasons both deceived the
other, she might have found some truth valuable to
herself and to others out of her experience. Instead
she ends by asking, "How did it end with YOU?" What
does this question mean? Is she really interested
in knowing how others' loves worked out? Is the
question covering up some other questions? Or does
she mean only to suggest her superior knowledge--that
love turned sour for her and will for others? Or is
she just a parading martyr?

The author of "Missing" doesn't say she has
gone up on a hill to shout her sadness or even that
she loved the boy she writes to, but the evidence come.
across very vividly that she knew him and cared for
him. Her love comes through so sensuously that many
readers will call to mind their past loves as well as
this girl's . . . so she does not have to say "I'm
sure you recognize my story/For it happened to you
too." There is no pose, no self-deception or reader-
deception here. The writer of "Sorrow" sounds as if
she is happy that a boy left her so she can parade
her anguish in public, and yet she writes what is
essentially a private statement that does not communicate why she even liked the boy. The writer of
"Missing" speaks memories that belonged to her but
in such a way the public share their memories with
the poem . . . she re-creates them instead of roman-
ticizing and philosophizing about them.

Exercise 4 - Writing a Memory Poem on Your Childhood:
O.K., now you try it--try writing for truth. Take
the memory you recorded in Exercise 2 and test it for
honesty. Eliminate anything that was put in to
impress anyone, especially yourself. Be true to
your memory by re-creating the facts of the experience.

For models or ideas of how to structure your
poem, here are some student memory poems:

PINK RIBBON PERFECT

Once there was a little girl
Who was very sweet.
She knew what to do
And how to act.
Everybody liked her.
Everybody loved her.

Sure, she was nice
And always acted right.
Compliments poured from
That smiling, smiling pink mouth.
She was everyone's friend
And oh, so cute when she was mad.

She was pink ribbon perfect.

Oh, yes, sometimes she was upset,
But only in the right manner.
Finally she tried oh, so hard
To tell someone how she felt
But they knew, oh, they knew
That she was just being cute again.
And so they laughed at her little stamping foot.

Do you know what happened
                        to that little girl?

She was gobbled up by her own mosters.
Yet even as she disappeared
Inside the red dragon's angry mouth,
She knew what to do
And how to act.
Everybody liked her.
Everybody loved her.
Everybody said
                goodbye
And forgot her the next shiny day

When another pink ribbon perfect came along.

                    --Cathy Cain
                    10th Grade

                    HAUNT

From the pages of a photo album
        she taunts me
                    in every class picture,

on the top row
        squeezed between the tallest boys.
Her nickname roar in my ears
                "too-tall . . . four-eyes".

Another picture found her--
                in the schoolroom doing math
                head leaning on hands, frowning
                always last to finish
                and late for lunch.

On another page she was laughing,
    it bubbled out uncontrolled
    at intervals between everyone else's
    receiving blank stares.

But in another album
    she had learned to wear the plaid uniform,
    it provided a sense of unity.
And in the class pictures
    they slowly grew up around her
    till she was only a face
    somewhere in the middle row.
She had applied a lipstick smile
    and plastic eyes
    (tinted blue).

From every photograph
    she swells up inside of me
    whispering . . . gently tormenting,
    telling me every horror story
    I long to forget

                    --Sharon Sandage
                      10th Grade

SING ME HOME

Way back when adulthood and boredom
Were merely abstract concepts,
I knew a girl-woman
Who played the sweetest guitar in the world.

They say opposites attract.
Well, she and I were opposite colors
In the family spectrum,
And although twelve years stretched between us,
We were like complementary colors.

When she played her guitar
And sang songs just for me,
She sang a shiny bubble.
I would crawl inside that bubble, and sit,
And laugh, and clap my hands gleefully
As I watched the world
Through iridescent bubble-colors.

That girl-woman did an awful thing:
She grew up,
Got married,
Had bubble-babies who shine
With iridescent colors.
Maybe tonight I'll call her up

And get her to sing me a song
About my childhood.

                              --Cathy Read
                                12th Grade

MAMA'S NOT NEVER COMING

mama's not never coming, i
worried, chirping within blumpy
blubbered cushions of a long rec-
tangular couch which was dark like
the large cagey room
that smuthered
it.

mama's not never coming, she forgot
Me and the thought knotted over in my
head sabbing, jutting
like each shiny cruel wood grain
facing parallel against
the four-year old
me.
roaring and freezing, the air con-
ditioner screamed behind my neck
and i felt hid-
den.

mama's not never going to pick me up
from this abandoned nursery, filled with
stale impartial furniture and
dark crowded
walls like
tired jurors.

mama doesn't care, you know, she doesn't
even like me, i think.
And the black sour
maid with inch-thick
ripples sticking out of her suit,
sneered
and I
    didn't matter anymore

as The Lysol floors and
                    lowering yellow outside
                    decided to not decide
        and   cared about not caring.

                              --Suzanne Stroud
                                12th Grade

Exercise 5 - Steppingstones of Your Life: You have just written a memory poem about your childhood, and to do so, you had to travel back over some roads of your life, retrace some steps, so to speak. Why did you choose to write about the experience you did? Because it was a moment you haven't forgotten--right? Right. Buy why haven't you forgotten it? Why was it significant enough to hang around in your memory all these years?

Not every memory is a significant one: probably some seem to be definitely more significant than others. For a while, let's concentrate on those significant ones, which Ira Profogg calls "The Steppingstones". Following is an adaptation of Progoff's exercise on steppingstones.

First, Progoff defines the steppingstones of your life as "those events that come to our minds when we spontaneously reflect on the course our life has taken . . . , the significant points of movement along the road of an individual's life.[11] To illustrate this idea, Progoff uses this example of Dag Hammarskjold's autobiographical book Markings:

> The metaphor that Hammarskjold uses is one that is natural to him as a lifelong mountain climber. The climber leaves markings behind as he proceeds up the mountain. But Hammarskjold points out that he does not leave markings only when he has gone upward. Sometimes the course takes him downward into a valley or ravine, and then it is equally important to leave a marker so that there is a record of the path that has been followed. In Hammarskjold's book he records all the variations of his climb up and down the mountain of his life; the same principle holds for our working with the exercises in the Steppingstones section. The Steppingstones are neutral with respect to pleasure or pain, progress or failure. They are simply the markings that are significant to use as we reconstruct the movement of our life.[12]

Do you understand the idea of the steppingstones? Good, then let's work with it but limit yourself to just the past two years instead of your entire life. To do this, Progoff suggests these steps:[13]

1. Get in a quiet, comfortable place where you will not be interrupted. Relax.

175

2. Let yourself travel in memory over the past two years. Allow yourself to simply feel the movement of your life. Recognize events, thoughts, feelings, but do not judge them or comment on them; merely observe, recall those events.

3. Now you are ready to begin listing your steppingstones. Since steppingstones are the most significant points in your past two years, you should limit them to ten. Progoff emphasizes that "spontaneous" selectivity is the essence of marking off your steppingstones.

4. Do not worry about getting your list in chronological order or about going into detail at this point. All that is required is a word or phrase--a note to yourself.

5. When your ten steppingstones are listed, relax, take a breather, then read over your list and ask yourself this question: What emotions and/or awarenesses arise in you as you do this? Write the answer to this question as an addendum to your steppingstones.

6. Next place your steppingstones in chronological order, starting with the events farthest into the past two years and ending with the most recent.

7. Now put flesh on the bones--fill in at least basic details for each event you listed as a steppingstone.

8. Finally, see if the list provides any pattern of experience in the past two years of your life. Does it give you a sense of motion, a moving context by which you might be able to "recognize implications and possibilities which lie . . . hidden" in the events of your life?

Hopefully, this steppingstones exercise will give you a process for dealing with your memories, and prepare you for the exercises to come!!

Memory: Time and Timelessness

Now that you've taken some trips back to your past, let's take a more in-depth look at time--

especially the past. First let's consider the nature of time--and timelessness.

There are times in our lives when time seems like a river carrying us ever more rapidly downstream, often against our will. The events in our lives seem like rocks or rapids or falls or drifting debris interspersed with gentle flowing in the sunlight. We can't avoid or hold onto these events; we are adrift in the time river, at the mercy of life's flow. And then there are moments when the flow is so pleasurable and joyous that our fear of passing time drives us to cling to the shore; we would like to stop time altogether.

However, these are not the only ways of relating to time. Have you ever been aware of being in the time river, and yet dwelling in <u>a space within yourself</u> that seems to be out of time? When we are simply in a place of awareness and equanimity that watches the river's flow, or the "passing show" with compassion, yet without losing perspective, without thinking that that is all there is; it is a dual perception of time that prophets and wisemen of all ages have pointed out as the bedrock of life lived consciously. It is a form of wisdom itself. Below is an exercise that will help you deepen your awareness of this dual perception of time:[14]

Exercise 6 - Creating the "Space-Surround":

Step 1: If you have one, get this year's calendar. If you don't simply recall the events of the last year. Think of the calendar as a horizontal time-line, stretching from past, now, future. Above the time line is space, below it is space.

	Space		
Time	<u>Past</u>	Now	Future
	Space		

Notice that all of these events on the calendar of your life, all events of time, <u>occur in</u> and are <u>surrounded</u> by space. This encircling, surrounding space is timeless, silent, and void--we'll call it the "space-surround".

Step 2: Now, from the events you have jotted on your calendar, or that you have stored in your memory, pick a past event, perhaps a joyous, fulfilling

experience that you wanted to cling to, you wanted
to make last, or one that was painful, one you
wanted to avoid. Bring into your mind the details of
the event itself--that is, whatever qualities, aspects,
feelings, or images of it arise. Stay with these
memories for a brief time, and then let them pass away,
until once again on the "space-surround". Allow your
mind to experience its timelessness, its quality of
being, an event surrounded by the formless quiet of
space.

Are you getting lost in all these abstracts?
It's easy to do! Let's make it more concrete: remember the metaphor we started with of your life as a
time stream, with the events of your life being rocks
or rapids or drifting debris in the river, and you
feeling adrift in this river, at the mercy of its
flow? In doing this exercise, imagine that the event
from the past year which you select to re-examine is,
say, a rock in the river. As you go back in memory,
you re-examine the rock in detail--all you know about
it, all your feelings about it, everything. In short,
you are in the river's flow, and through memory, you
again either want to avoid that rock, if it represents
a painful or fearful experience, or you want to cling
to it, if it represents a pleasurable, fulfilling
event. Now, when you begin to shift to the "space-
surround", you actually get out of the time-river,
and you are on the river bank, looking at the rock.
Only from the bank can you see the rock for what it
is: Only one separate event in the river, one among
many. But in the river, clinging to that rock, or
frantically trying to avoid it, all you can think
of is that rock! Get the point? The "space-surround"--
getting distance from the bank--puts each of life's
events into perspective: It gives us an objectivity
we can't have as long as we are caught in the river
trying to deep from drowning.

Another way of making this abstract/concept,
"the space-surround", more concrete is by visualizing
it this way:

                    Space

                (Riverbank)

    Time-

    River   Past ──────→ Now ─────────→ Future

                (Riverbank)

                    Space

As you watch each event of the past year, each rock, each floating twig and leaf, each deep-flowing quiet pool, each shallow place in your time-river, notice that each has a beginning, middle, and end, when viewed from the riverbank, the "space-surround", but only from the bank can you see it; caught in the river, it is much harder to see it in perspective. Standing on the riverbank, you can view a series of past events, experiencing each event as it appears, is present, and then disappears, like telephone poles passing close by the window of a moving car. Have you ever stood on a riverbank, simply watching the river flow--and observed a leaf there, a log caught on a rock there, a paper cup there--and on and on? Memory, when viewed from the "space-surround," functions just like that.

The more you practice viewing time and life's events like this, the more you see that into the center of the "space-surround" pass the events of your life--thought after thought, feeling after feeling, experience after experience--each arising, existing, and flowing on. This awareness will help free you from identifying with the part of yourself that is caught in time, or in the river-flow, and you will find yourself not only free from the fear of time, but a joyous participant in the flow of life.

Step 3: Now, let's put this new perspective into practice through writing. Using this event from last year which you selected in Step 1, jot down as many details, feelings, sense impressions and facts as you can remember. Try to re-create the event in words, so that your readers may experience it with you. Then pull away from the event into the "space-surround"; get out of the river and stand on the bank, and look at it objectively, as simply one event in the time-river flow. Then, from that perspective, write the experience into a poem or short narrative.

Below are some student examples:

TAKING TURNS

We sprawled on the cement steps,
    The sun dappling our legs,
    Drinking cold Schlitz,
    Arguing endlessly.

Taking turns buying beer,
    Taking turns winning arguments,
    Taking turns saying "I love you".
We mellowed a hot summer.

Now when I think of you,
    I taste Schlitz.
But that was a year ago,
    And I still hate to take turns.

                    --Charlie Moore
                      12th Grade

SCREAM WOMAN

I

If pen and ink could be
Bullet and gun
I'd blast the balls off
The one who made me
Hate,
Who made me
Afraid,
Who made me
Cold.

II

I can hear his voice echo
"Pretty girl, pretty pretty girl,
I'm so glad you came out tonight . . .
I've been waiting at your window,
The shadow you thought was a tree;
Pretty, pretty girl . . ."

III

Scream, woman,
Until your lungs are
Black and blue,
Until your face contorts
To red
And your eyes turn
Gray and glassy.
Scream, but no words
Can soothe
Your brutal wounds,
Because the scars burn
Forever.

                    --Karen King
                      12th Grade

ALL SAINT'S DAY

Yesterday was Halloween:
a day for fun
        for tapping time
in triplets

slowing
the time signature
into uneven
drawnout quarter notes
of atonal timbre.

People switched roles
took off their masks
accented parts of their character
that had remained forgotten
in past lives.

But I was dressed as usual
afraid to unveil myself
before joking, rhythmical eyes.
I sat there,
smiling with them;
or was I really
smiling at them
        and
                myself?

And on the bus going home
I passed other people
like me
dressed in ordinary, everyday clothes.
Were they too
scared to smile
and laugh loudly
at simply nothing?
When will I ever learn
to catch those moments.
When I too
reeled around my world
happy
just to be living
        and breathing?
Maybe I was too caught up with my experiences
to bottle them
        or
I was too afraid
they would be categorized.

I've missed something
by not taking the Promethean leap of
holding time, syncopated
in my quivering fingers.

                        --Phoebe Jewell
                        12th Grade

MARCH

There's a type of day that comes in March
When the sky rears up like a fish from the depths
And boys bait it with kites.

It toys with the string a moment
Then pulls you up there in its mouth
And as a kite--
You feel as if one more gust might shatter you
As if, breathless, you might plunge to earth--
But you dance,
You dance a tightrope-step between life and death,
There in the empty sky.
As a diamond breathed to a life no crystal knows
By the breath of the sun.

Hours later the kites are drawn in, their lines
    wound,
Their frames hitched to bikes or toted.
Boys press their aching craned necks
And talk after so long a quiet.
The kites float from their backs, protest,
    struggle to soar;
Each has wings.

Men with pudgy faces finish their fish eggs
And wipe their fingers on napkins.

                    --Tom Garvey
                    12th Grade

Step 4: O.K., for more practice, repeat
the process of Step 3, but this time, select an
event from last week to develop into a poem or a
short narrative.

Below is an imaginative treatment of one
student's reaction to a party he had attended:

BLACK FOREST--THURSDAY AT 8

The wart hog sat quietly, turning his gin
and tonic slowly in his thick callous hands.
He leaned back in his chair and anchored his
right foot on his left knee while the cocktail
party swirled ambiguously around his small
corner.

Beavers, crablice, dogs, mantis, antelope,
cats, beetles, and the like floated about the
long dining room talking merrily or dancing
cheek-to-cheek, or mandible to feeler or jowl
to tusk or what have you. In any case, the

ladies paraded long silken evening gowns
and high featured hats topped with brocade
and lace and perhaps a flower. The men, as
was the warthog, were decked out in the
finest tuxedos of black and grey. The tinkle
of glasses and the soft hum of the musicians
filled the rooms, broken only by a periodic
high wailing scream as the mantis invited
another of the slightly thick fly sisters out
dancing on the balcony. As he sat next to
high french windows, the warthog viewed the
struggle outside which culminated in the
smiling mantis tugging the head off the 43rd
fly sister and tossing it among the 42 others.

The warthog turned back around and straight
ened his tie as a radiant young female hawk
arrived and placed herself carefully into the
only other chair in his corner.

"Good evening," she said dipping her head.

"Uh hello," he returned, being at this point
quite drunk. "Uh, how do you do?"

"Quite nicely thank you," she said and began
to rummage noisily in a medium-sized black bag,
emerging with a pack of Virginia Slims and a
lighter. "These lighters confuse me so. Uh,
would you mind greatly . . . ?" She held out
the lighter.

He took it, lit the smoke, and handed her a
drink. A wild roar broke loose followed by a
loud crash as a badger pushed a large china
cabinet onto a pair of Irish Fox Hounds.

"This is the first of these Black Forest
functions I've been to," she chirped, "I've never
had such fun."

The badger burst into the room, jumped over
a couch, knocked over side tables, an old tree
squirrel, and dashed out the door, a third fox
hound close at his heels. Battle ensued on the
front lawn.

The warthog sipped his drink, "It must be
lousy having a lot of hereditary enemies."

"Yes, I sometimes wonder why those palatable
looking little mice ever come to those things.
They make me quite nervous. I've always been
nervous, you know."

183

"For your information, madam, I've known few hawks who weren't schizophrenic."

"Do you suppose it's our upbringing?"

"Can't say really."

"Well, I just hope they don't come near. I'm afraid I'd soil my dress."

"Sure . . . Have another?"

"Thank you." She took the martini that he had grabbed from a passing pig waiter.

Two Rocky Mountain spotted fever ticks were working their way up the warthog's pantleg. He reached down and picked the two off his leg and dropped them into a martini where they mounted an olive and spent the evening taking dips or trying to attract the cocktail waiter's attention.

"I wonder, sometimes, if we'll ever break loose from old mother nature . . . fighting and killing. Jesus! I get damn sick of it sometimes. My mother, God bless 'er, once told me never to attack anything I wasn't planning to eat. It's a hell of philosophy. I have few enemies and ninety percent of those are plants, anyway. I live an easy life."

She looked at him for a moment making a funny clicking sound through her smooth grey beak. Then she glanced out the window and chuckled, "Yes, Mister Warthog, I believe you do." She smiled. "I just wish things were the same for me, though. I can't get far on vegetables, you know." She looked at him. "I believe someone wishes to speak to you."

At that moment a bedraggled badger charged the warthog from behind the grand drape.

The warthog moving much faster than one would expect from a pig, and a very large pig at that, jumped up and side-stepped Ed the badger. The badger flew past the warthog and crashed through the french window, hitting the balcony with his hips and flipping over the rail to fall to the front lawn. An iridescent sparkle of broken glass followed him down to the soft turf. The badger got up and hobbled back in the front door.

The hawk stood up and straightened her gown.
She picked up her drink. The warthog sat panting
and wheezing.

"Well, sir, have a good evening. Perhaps
we'll speak again tonight."

"Oh . . . us . . . yah, g'nite." The hawk
held out her hand, averting her eyes for a few
moments and then, looking back, noticed that the
warthog had wandered to the bar.

--Mark Greene
12th Grade

Exercise 7 - To Bottle Time: In his book, Dandelion
Wine, Ray Bradbury develops the metaphor of making
summer dandelion wine as a way of teaching the lesson that "bottling time" is a valuable and important
process. The young boy, who is the book's main character, spends much of the summer picking dandelions,
preparing and making the wine, so that in the cold,
sunless winter months, he can go into the collar, pull
a bottle from the shelf labelled July 18th, and
re-experience the warmth, sunshine, and beauty of that
July day.

Writing, too, is a way to bottle time, a more
difficult, painstaking way, granted, but much less
alcoholic! Have some people been so important to your
life that you wanted to preserve them, "bottle" them,
so you could re-experience them at another time and
place? Instead of putting them in a bottle (that is
so uncomfortable--and a bit cruel?), let's try to put
them into words--exactly who that person is, and
what it was they gave you, and still give you each
time you think of them . . . ? Below are student poems
which attempt to capture in words a significant
person in one's life.

to brother kevin: BEAUTIFUL BOY-CHILD

beautiful boy-child, i watch you as the days
        go past,
wanting to run faster than your short, stout
        legs can carry you,
tossing me your brilliant three-year old grin
        as you
defiantly do exactly what i tell you not to,
holding you against my breast, your warm arms
        encircling
my neck. why must you grow up?

185

you come to me with skinned hands and a tear-
      stained,
muddy face wanting me to kiss it and make it
      all better.

beautiful boy-child, i watch you as the days
      turn into
months and the months turn into years.
you're growing taller and you don't come to me
      anymore
with tears because big boys don't cry.

pretty-boy . . . that's what they used to call
      you, isn't it?
and so you push back the tears and hide behind
      clenched
fists. your anger and tough exterior conceal
      your soft
eyes and shy smile. . . . i once knew a boy
      like you,
but they got to him too. he hid behind shoulder-
      pads and
basketballs and a varsity letter M (it stood for
      masculinity)
and as i watch you, i think of him.

beautiful boy-child, every time i see you, my
      heart dies
a little more. i watch them form you and mold
      you.
they take you apart and assemble you into
      someone i
don't know. they take you away and force you to
      become a man.

                        --Laureen McGehee
                          12th Grade

OH, BRAVE HERACLES

On a dark playground,
Near an empty schoolhouse,
She looked for her Christmas ring.

He offered to help,
Showed her "two ways to pray":
                  on her knees,
                  face and hands up,
                  pleading to a non-existent
                                  god,

Or on her back,
Legs spread wide,

Shorts around her knees.
    (She was only ten.)

Her child-screams frightened him off.
She dried her tears,
Straightened her clothes,
                and found her way home.
For four years,
            for fear of ridicule or shame,
She said nothing,
            only stayed away from the dark.
    (She never found her ring).

Like brave Heracles,
He stole her only tooth,
                and only eye.

                    --Eric Coleman
                    10th Grade

TOUGH BOY

Look at me, tough boy.
Don't tell me what you think,
Hand me a line.
Toss your head defiantly
To get the hair out of your eyes.
Keep your arms taut like an ape, by your sides
Ready to spring into a punch.

Look at me, tough boy.
Hate me 'cause when
I touch you, you're gonna cringe like a shy
        animal.
And I am gonna touch you.
You can't run though.
That'd be chicken.
Stay here and fight
With my weapons.

Look at me, tough boy.
I'm gonna smooth the hair
Out of your eyes
With my soft fingers.
I'm gonna touch you
        and take you
        and break you
            and make you
                    Look at me.

                    --Elizabeth Plaag
                    12th Grade

The following two poems were written to a classmate
who, a few months before, had committed suicide:

PORTRAIT

Not one of the nameless
Nor one of the faceless,
But one I never gave
                    a second glance.
They saw you as peaceful.
They said you were
        a country kitchen
        a yellow pinto
        a stuffy animal . . .
Their three guesses were up
        and they were wrong,
                    I guess.
And now they're all wondering
        why so much pain?
                    Why?
Those who play by the rules
        casting their fools
        drown in talk and romance . . .
    They go on . . . getting by . . .
                next time
                    I'll
                        take
                that second glance.

                    --Rachel Jones
                        12th Grade

ENDING

Alone in the crowd,
She was deaf to the few
Who shouted at her through the haze.
No matter how hard they shouted,
The sound waves were still not strong enough
To break down the barriers.

To some, her eyes screamed for
Help,
But were blind
To the soul-searching gazes
Of those who saw,
And she drew her opaque eyelids closed
Like black window shades.

She was blind,
So she groped in the darkness
And pricked her small, soft fingers
Again and again.

188

When she finally touched something warm
And receptive,
She recoiled from the terrible unfamiliarity
Of the moment.

And so she went home.
Quietly shut her door in the world's face,
Locked it,
And to make sure
It would never be opened again,
She swallowed the key.

> --Cathy Read
> 12th Grade

Empathy--Another Way of Experiencing Imaginatively

Are you familiar with the word empathy?
Webster's defines it like this:

> em-pa-thy/'em-pe-the/N.1: the imaginative
> projection of a subjective state into an
> object so that the object appears to be
> infused with it. 2: the capacity for parti-
> cipating in another's feelings or ideas.

All of us have felt empathy, haven't we? All of us
have identified ourselves with a person or an object
so strongly that we participated in that person's
emotional and even physical sensations. Can you
think of some empathic experiences you've had? Have
you ever been at a movie, for example, and gotten
so involved with a character that you found yourself
smiling when he laughed, crying when he cried, even
dodging when something was thrown at him?

How is empathy different from sympathy?
Hmmm . . . yes, the distinction is subtle, but very
important. Sympathy usually includes a trace of
pity--which involves one person, outside of and in a
more advantageous, perhaps a more safe and less painful, position, than another--and that person is
almost above the one being sympathized with. Empathy,
on the other hand, is the projection of self into
the place of another. Holman points out that the
word is a translation of Einfuhlung, meaning "feeling
into"--which is quite different from sympathy, meaning
to feel pity or compassion for.[15] Empathy is being
one, an identification: "I am you." Sympathy keeps
the distance, the division between two people: "I,
separate from you, feel for you."

189

Empathy, then, is a way of experiencing, of responding, of feeling, and of seeing; it is a way that imaginatively conditions experience and personalizes the otherwise impersonal, a way of fusing, thus centering the outer and inner worlds. For the writer, empathy is crucial to interest and to involve readers. The following exercises are intended to develop your powers of empathy:

Exercise 8 - A Typical Day in the Life of--: As children, most of us endowed a doll, a pencil, a baseball, bat, or some object with special, individual, human powers. Get into that mindset again. Select an inanimate object--any object--then empathize. Become that object, endow the object with human powers; it has all our senses, feelings, dreams, hopes, and fears. Experience what happens in the typical day of your object; experience what it feels and senses--and tell us your story.

To get you warmed up, do this exercise: Pretend that you are a building. Be specific and exact about the building you choose. Write on a piece of paper the building you have chosen. Now answer these questions:

1. Can you breathe?
2. Do you look like the buildings around you?
3. Could your architect have done a better job? How?
4. Do birds like you?
5. What will happen to you when an earthquake hits?
6. Are you attractive?
7. Do you block people's views?
8. Can you see any trees around you?
9. Are you kept in good condition?
10. Do you show your age?
11. Do you get sunshine?
12. Do people who live and work inside you like you?
13. What is going on inside you?

O.K.--that should get you into an empathetic mood. Now write out "A typical day in the life of--" in either diary, short narrative or narrative verse form.

Below are some professional poems which provide interesting models for empathy with an inanimate object.

190

THE CAULIFLOWER

I want to be a cauliflower,
all brain and ears,
meditating on the origin of gardens
and the divinity of Him
who carefully binds my leaves.

With my blind roots touched
by the songs of the worms,
and my rough throat throbbing
with strange, vegetable sounds,
perhaps I'd feel the parting stroke
of a butterfly's wing . . .

Not like those cousins the cabbages,
whose heads, tightly folded,
see and hear nothing of this world,
dreaming only on the yellow
and green magnificence
that is hardening within them.[16]

STONE

Go inside a stone
That would be my way.
Let somebody else become a dove
Or gnash with a tiger's tooth.
I am happy to be a stone.

From the outside the stone is a riddle:
No one knows how to answer it.
Yet within, it must be cool and quiet
Even though a cow steps on it full weight,
Even though a child throws it in a river;
The stone sinks, slow, unperturbed
To the river bottom
Where the fishes come to knock on it
And listen.

I have seen sparks fly out
When two stones are rubbed,
So perhaps there is a moon shining
From somewhere, as though behind a hill--
Just enough light to make out
The strange writings, the star-charts
On the inner walls.[17]

                              --Charles Simic

The following poem presents itself as a riddle,
which might be an approach that appeals to you more
than "A typical day in the life of--". If so, take

the riddle approach instead. The exercise in empathy
is the same.

MONEY

At first it will seem tame,
willing to be domesticated.

It will nest
in your pocket
or curl up in a corner
reciting softly to itself
the names of the presidents.

It will delight your friends,
shake hands with men
like a dog and lick
the legs of women.

But like an amoeba
it makes love
in secret
only to itself.

Its food is normal
American food.
Fold it frequently;
it needs exercise.

Water it every three days
and it will repay you
with displays of affection.

Then one day when you think
you are its master
it will turn its head
as if for a kiss
and bite you gently
on the hand.

There will be no pain
but in thirty seconds
the poison will reach your heart.[18]

                          --Victor Contoski

Exercise 9 - Jumping into Another's Place: Now apply
your imagination and empathy to a person instead of
an object. Get into someone else's head and situation. Not only has a great deal of excellent literature been written through this technique (where would
Mark Twain have been if he hadn't been able to become
a boy named Huck Finn--or a different one named
Tom Sawyer?!!!!), but if we could develop the art of

empathy, our human relationships would tremendously improve. Consider the impact of empathy on our daily quarrels! Try this exercise and see:[19]

Step 1: Isolate yourself in a quiet place at a time when you feel fairly well and have a certain measure of control over your emotions. Get comfortable. Lean back and close your eyes. Now recall a specific incident involving a person with whom you often quarrel or have friction of some kind. Begin to see and feel that specific quarrel. Hear the dialogue from beginning to end. Feel the temperature. See the surroundings, the setting of the quarrel. Make yourself go all the way through the experience. Stop trying to win the argument; drop that effort completely.

Instead, with a leap of the imagination, jump into the other person's place. In order to do this, you must for the moment put yourself aside. This is not easy. Quietly, determinedly and surely, take the whole of yourself, good and bad feelings, thoughts, ideas, sensations, and put them away somewhere--just for a while. Don't worry; there is no danger of losing them--.

If you are having difficulty jumping into another's place by a simple leap of imagination, try this approach: Imagine yourself sitting or standing or walking just as the other person is doing. Imagine your face expressing what his face expresses, your hands moving just as his move. You feel as he feels; you are the other person. You think what he thinks, say what he says; you feel your heart beating like his. You see you, hear your voice and your words as he does. Now, again, go through the same quarrel. You are the other person; you see yourself as he sees you and you see him as he sees himself because you are now the other person.

Step 2: It is one thing to accomplish this "becoming someone else" in solitude and privacy. It is another thing to jump into the other's place in the heat of the argument or quarrel. But the exercise will help. Even if we can enter into the other's world just a little, how much more intelligently we can deal with him--how much less wounded and disturbed we will be by his actions and words. In your journal, write a response or reaction to this exercise--even if it is only a summary. Here are two samples of reactions to this exercise that were later developed into poems:

YOU'LL BE THE SAME WAY . . .

"on the phone again I
see you haven't finished your homework
don't be smart with me and
change your bad attitude
wipe that smile away
cause your room's a mess and why
lock yourself in there
you're never home and you treat
us like we're a stop and go
live with your father
always spoiled you don't
understand how I feel
but you'll be the same way
when you quit acting like a child and
act your age and hang up that phone now!"

She exhaled. And brushed a wisp of sprayed hair from her damp eyes.

--Sharon Sandage
11th Grade

LISTEN MY SON . . .

"Listen my son and you shall hear
The midmorning beating and kick in the rear.
I don't know where you've gone wrong.
I've given you everything you've wanted.
I've tried with you.
You're a failure.
You're no good.
Your mother's not much better.
You've plotted against me.
You've blotted me out.
What are you doing tonight?
Why are you always gone?
You should be home studying.
I've been waiting for a signal of change.
Turn yourself around 180 degrees.
Do this.
Do that.
Don't do this.
Don't do that.
BITCH, BITCH, BITCH, BITCH, BITCH."

The boy understood perfectly why
his father had the heart attack, he just didn't
know why it hadn't happened sooner.

--Alex Georges
10th Grade

Exercise 10 - Persona Poems: Now that you have some
experience in jumping into another person's place,
let's try to write some persona poems. Persona is a
literary term which, very simply, refers to the nar-
rator of the poem. It literally means a mask and
refers to the "second self" created by the poet
and through whose eyes the poem's content is seen.
In writing a persona poem, you literally become a
"second self," become the person in the poem. The
process is simple: You pretend you are someone else,
get into the situation, the head and heart, and then
speak through that person. Here are two persona
poems by the poet Jane Shore to use as models. In
the first poem, "Ararat," the persona is Noah's
wife. The flood had receded, the ark is perched on
Mt. Ararat, and she speaks her feelings:

ARARAT

Somebody said the sea would come to us
cutting like an army through wheat--
its captive women, dolphins in the wake
of our little boat. As water drains
every wife's a sea-wife. Such traffic
you would think it market day!
Hooked to their elbows, baskets
of apricots and limes,
anchor the windows in the muddy slopes
where the world begins. The elements
have never been more married.

I have grown to love tending this garden
that barks and coos in the moonlight
when there is a moon.
Spindly giraffes cluster at the bow.
Ants inch down the plank in twos.
The sheep are nervous. Their thick wool
steams as the dew burns off.

Crises crush men more. In sleep
my husband's pitchy hands hammer the air
as if another boat could float us back
to who we were. I imagine

I am the mountain he teeters on
as every wave of wind comes past.
I watch for clouds.[20]

                    --Jane Shore

In the next poem, a lifeguard who is tormented by
those who have drowned is the persona:

THE LIFEGUARD

The children vault the giant carpet roll
of waves, with sharp cries swing legs
wide over water. A garden of umbrellas
blooms down the stretch of beach. Far
offshore always I can spot that same
pale thumbprint of a face going under,
grown bigger as I approach, the one arm circling,
locking rigid around my neck. The other
as its fist hooks and jabs my head away.
Ear to the conch, ear to the pillow,
beneath a canopy of bathers each night
I hear the voice and pry the jaws apart,
choke on the tangle of sable hair that blurs
the dead girl's mouth: that anarchy
of breath dog-soft and still at my neck.
She calls from the water glass I drink from.
From my own throat when I swallow.[21]

                    --Jane Shore

Get the idea? Now you try it. Select anyone you
wish as your persona. You might choose a historical
figure from the past--a prophet, or a great artist,
musician, scientist, or leader; or you might choose
someone from your own life. Here is a student's
persona poem on the artist Mark Rothko.

ARTIST
(The Rothko Chapel)

Let me play for you
     I'll play your song
        Let me paint for you
     You'll love the colors
                    Let me tell you a story
     You love happy endings
But
        don't ask me if you can listen
                            when I play for
                            myself
I never hang my absentminded doodles
                        in the Louvre

196

When my words are words of fear
                        you won't hear
                        them if I can help
                        it
Because these are the songs my mind plays for me
                        late at night
                        when lights are out
        And these ultraviolet murals
            are for my eyes only
                too sacred.

                        --David McLaughlin
                        11th Grade

If you still don't have any ideas, you might look at
some good human interest photographs and become one
of the people in the photograph. There is only one
requirement: Become someone else, then speak through
that person, experience that person's situation--ima-
ginatively.

Allusion: A Connection Between Memory and Empathy

        Throughout most of this chapter, we have been
dealing with using imagination and insight as a tool
to "connect" the world of our experience (the world
of the senses, the "now" universe), with the world
of our memory (the past), with the world of emotion
(our feelings, empathy).

        The literary device of allusion is a technique
which seems a "natural" to bring all of those elements
together. At the very least, allusion is a way of
using the experience of others imaginatively to vivify
and enlarge our own experience.

        What is allusion? Don't confuse it with
illusion. An allusion may be defined as a reference
to another literary work, to another art form, to
historical events or personalities, to mythology,
to popular and contemporary personalities and events. [22]
In short, allusion is a way of making a connection
between what you are writing about (what you are
experiencing in the "now" universe) and what your
reader has read before or heard about. You see? To
bring these two fields of experience (yours and your
reader's) together is an act of imagination, insight,
and empathy, an act of balance, of centering.

197

Here are some points you need to consider
in using the technique of allusion:

The success of an allusion will depend on
whether you strike a responsive chord in your
reader's memory. After all, the reader must
be able to recognize what you are alluding to.
So choose an allusion that will fit your audience; let some word or phrase, or even your
very style, refer to or suggest a similarity
between the subject you are discussing and
the thing you are alluding to. The success
of the use of allusion, according to the
Princeton Encyclopedia of Poetry and Poetics,
assumes:

(1) An established literary tradition as a
source of value; (2) an audience sharing the
tradition with the poet; (3) an echo of suf-
ficiently familiar yet distinctive and meaningful elements; and (4) a fusion of the echo
with elements in a new context.[23]

In other words, allusion requires the readers' fami-
liarity with the original for full understanding and
appreciation, but placed in the context of your
present experience.

Exercise 1 - Allusions in Popular Music: One of the
most easily accessible sources of allusions in art
today is popular music. Listen to and study the
lyrics of the following music in regard to use of
allusion: Look especially closely at the way the music
fuses the object or event being alluded to with the
present experience of the songwriter. That is the
heart of the allusion. What does this past event say
to me now?

Music using literary allusions:
"Goodbye Yellow Brick Road" by Elton John
"Guinevere" by Crosby, Stills, Nash and
    Young on So Far
"Don Quixote" by Gordon Lightfoot
"House at Pooh Corner" by Loggins and Messina
"The Tales of Horror/Fall of the House of
    Usher" by Allan Parsons

Music using historical allusions:
"Pancho and Lefty" (The legend of the death
    of Pancho Villa) by Emmy Lou Harris,
    Luxury Liner

198

"Vincent" by Don McLean (tribute to Vincent
   van Gogh)
"American Pie" (on the death of Buddy Holly)
   by Don McLean
"Amelia" (on the life/death of Amelia
   Earhart) by Joni Mitchell
"Elvis and Marilyn" by Leon Russell,
   Americana
"Roy Rogers" by Elton John, Yellow Brick
   Road
"Candle in the Wind" (a tribute to Marilyn
   Monroe) by Elton John, Yellow Brick Road
"War of the Worlds" (radio show)

Music using mythic/symbolic allusions:
"The Eagle Will Rise Again" by Allan Parsons,
   Pyramid
"Pegasus" by John Denver
"Jericho" by Joni Mitchell, Don Juan's
   Reckless Daughter
"Woodstock" by Joni Mitchell

Did an examination of the music clarify for you how
allusions work? Do you see that the use of allusion
enriches our awareness of our own experience? It
gives a deeper, richer layer of understanding to our
experience because it puts it in a new context, a
context which merges our experience with the experience of the great events and people of the past.

Exercise 2 - Use of Allusion in Poetry: Actually
the process of writing an allusion is simply the act
of fusing the event or person you are alluding to
with your present situation or experience. Graphic-
ally, it looks like this:

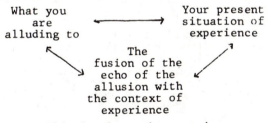

This is where the poem is.

For example, consider May Sarton's poem below:

THE MUSE AS MEDUSA

I saw you once, Medusa; we were alone.
I looked you straight in the cold eye, cold.
I was not punished, was not turned to stone--
How to believe the legends I am told?

I came as naked as any little fish,
Prepared to be hooked, gutted, caught;
But I saw you, Medusa, made my wish,
And when I left you I was clothed in thought . . .

Being allowed, perhaps, to swim my way
Through the great deep and on the rising tide,
Flashing wild streams, as free and rich as they,
Though you had power marshalled on your side.

The fish escaped to many a magic reef;
The fish explored many a dangerous sea--
The fish, Medusa, did not come to grief,
But swims still in a fluid mystery.

Forget the image: your silence is my ocean,
And even now it teems with life. You chose
To abdicate by total lack of motion,
But did it work, for nothing really froze?

It is all fluid still, that world of feeling
Where thoughts, those fishes, silent, feed and
    rove;
And, fluid, it is also full of healing,
For love is healing, even rootless love.

I turn your face around! It is my face.
That frozen rage is what I must explore--
Oh secret, self-enclosed, and ravaged place!
This is the gift I thank Medusa for.[24]

                    --May Sarton

    Let's apply this poem to the graph above:

1. What is the poem alluding to? Obviously
    the Greek myth of Medusa, the fearsome god-
    dess of great beauty, but who was most
    horrible to mortals; whoever looked on her
    beauty was turned instantly to stone. To
    understand and appreciate Sarton's poem,
    this is all the reader really needs to know
    about the myth.

2. How does Sarton echo the distinctive and
    meaningful details of the allusion? Which
    lines in the poem jog the reader's memory,

cause the "echo"? Look at the first stanza:
"I saw you once Medusa; we were alone./I
looked you straight in the cold eye, cold./
I was not punished, was not turned to stone--".

3. What is the situation or experience, the
personal context into which Sarton fuses the
allusion to Medusa? She gives us a strong
hint in the title--the muse as Medusa . . .
ahhh--Sarton, the poet, sees her muse, her
inspiration for writing as a power as fear-
some, as cold as Medusa, who when confronted,
can turn her to stone, leave her lifeless,
unable to write! But that is still the echo
of the allusion, isn't it?

4. What experience does the poem describe? The
poem is about a different kind of experience
with the muse, this Medusa. . . . Sarton
says in the second stanza: "I came naked
as any little fish/Prepared to be hooked,
gutted, caught;/But when I saw you, Medusa,
made my wish,/And when I left you I was
clothed in thought." Ah--the confrontation
with Medusa was an inspiration, the poet
"swims still in a fluid mystery" from the
encounter, was not frozen into stone.

5. And what was the significance of this experience, this allusion? Sarton's last stanza
says it very carefully: "I turn your face
around! It is my face./That frozen rage is
what I must explore--/Oh secret, self-enclosed,
and ravaged place!/This is the gift I thank
Medusa for." Wow--it is that moment of
realization when she sees her muse, her
inspiration for writing, is that secret,
self-enclosed "ravaged place" of "frozen
rage"--Medusa.

Now look at the following poems as further models for
fusing the allusion with the context of your own
experience.

AT DELPHI

The site echoes
Its own huge silences

Wherever one stands,
Whatever one sees--

Narrow terror of the pass
Or its amazing throat,
Pouring an avalanche of olives
Into the blue bay.

Crags so fierce
They nearly swallow
A city of broken pillars,
Or Athene's temple,

Exquisite circle,
Gentled on all sides
By silvery leaves.

Eagles floating
On high streamers of wind,
Or that raw cleft,
Deep in the rock,
Matrix
Where the oracle
Uttered her two-edged words.

Wherever one stands,
Every path leads to Fate itself:
"Speak! Speak!"

But there is no answer.

Choose the river of olives.
Choose the eagles.
Or choose to balance
All these forces,
The violent, the gentle;
Summon them like winds
Against a lifted finger.
Choose to be human.

Everyone stands here
And listens. Listens.
Everyone stands here alone.

I tell you the gods are still alive
And they are not consoling.

I have not spoken of this
For three years,
But my ears still boom.[25]

                              --May Sarton

THE OTHER GARDEN

the ram in the sacred tree
mounts up happily
his lapis lazuli eyes
squint in paradise
his tail quivering

his body thin hammered gold
a face centuries old
few-bearded, satisfied

the simply flower of the tree
bright with emerald leaves
droops aside

his horny feet knocking
he plows his chosen bride

Evoe! Evoe!
the garden (again) is sanctified.[26]

--John Gill

NARCISSUS

His eyes are darker than he knows.
They flash out from a fire so deep
It draws him down to burning shadows.
It draws him further down than sleep.
And there in any quiet room
He faces a peculiar doom.
Within the mirror's empty face
His own eyes dreadfully expose
His solitary self, that place
He cannot leave, he cannot reach.
Whatever mirrors have to teach
He will learn now before he moves,
Lost in himself, but far from love.

It is not love that makes him fall
Deep into perilous reflection,
Not love that holds him there at all,
But rather something glimpsed and gone,
Angels and unicorns he sees
Vanish among the little trees,
Their lives so innocent and wise
That draw him into his own eyes,
Those fleeting selves that come quite near
But never tell him who they are.

He knew that he can never leave
Without the gift they have to give,
Powers that he must catch and tame
Or, drawn into the mirror, drown.[27]

--May Sarton

THE RETURN OF APHRODITE

Under the wave it is altogether still,
Alive and still, as nourishing as sleep,
Down below conflict, beyond need or will,
Where love flows on and yet is there to keep,
As unconstrained as waves that lift and break
And their bright foam neither to give nor take.

Listen to the long rising curve and stress,
Murmur of ocean that brings us the goddess.

From deep she rises, poised upon her shell.
O guiltless Aphrodite so long absent!
The green waves part. There is no sound at all
As she advances, tranquil and transparent,
To lay on mortal flesh her sacred mantle.

The wave recedes--she is drawn back again
Into the ocean where light leaves a stain.[28]

--May Sarton

Exercise 3 - Writing Allusion Poems: Now it is time
for you to try your hand (and mind) at building a
poem around allusion. You really should try writing
at least four allusion poems: (1) one concentrating
on an allusion to a Greek myth; (2) one on allusion
to a historical event or famous person from the past;
(3) one using an allusion to a piece of literature or
an author; and (4) one an allusion to a contemporary
event or famous person that made an impact on you in
your own lifetime. Below are some student allusion
poems you might use as models:

MEDUSA

She sits by her mirror
Admiring herself,
A cosmetics clutter before her,
And she's still white . . .
And cold . . .

More paint, never enough paint,
So pale, so coarse.
"Colors, I need more colors" she screams
At her distorted image . . .

Lady, it's not your face
That shows no life . . .
        It's your blank and empty eyes
                    That see none.

Frozen Medusa
                    Admires herself.

                    --Julie Lee
                      10th Grade

JFK'S ASSASSINATION

"Twas the shot seen around the world"
And they mourned their silver-coated God
Who came with white teeth flashing.
"How could he die?" they asked themselves,
And crying into cloth coats
                    watched the instant replay.
They wondered why the widow jumped
        When all of him
                    hit all of her.

I would,
        wouldn't you?

I've seen that ride a hundred times.
I guess I should've cried
                    or something.
But I just sat with morbid fascination
And wondered why they didn't get
                        a
                        clearer
                            picture.

                    --Cathy Cain
                      10th Grade

GREEK GODS TO LIE

You have deceived me, Eurydice.
You cowered in my shadow as I walked on . . .
                through the forests of grey faces,
                through clouded waters, past
                    bloodied bayonets stabbing the
                                        sky,
Until the thorns in my feet became angry welts.
Yet, I kept walking,
                humming my dark thoughts into
                    streams of song.
    My path did not stray.
I never tasted the bitterness of birch bark or
                touched the skins laced with
                            black cancer.

205

```
                cries of dying whales screamed past my
                                    ears . . .
I just hummed louder.
But, my welts grew redder, gathered pus, and my
                                    walk faltered.
I no longer heard the soft tread of you,
                    Eurydice, behind me.
I turned for reassurance, a gentle touch,
        but you, like a detestable yellow slug
                                    crawled away.
I knelt,
        carefully plucking the first thorn.
            I knew I couldn't just walk past anymore.

                            --Christine Kim
                              10th Grade
```

ATHENA

```
Pounding away inside
                she bruises and tears,
Battling through layers
                of intellect, logic and calm,
Through the hard shell
                of skull.
Feeding her supression
                    just makes her stronger
                            and angrier--
She grows double strength for every
Setback she takes;
It grows harder
                to control such a
                        violent warrior.
(Within she beats, screams, and demands
                    to be heard.)
Athena
    will explode soon;
                I see the thin lines
                        of cracks.

                            --Karen King
                              12th Grade
```

All right. Hopefully, by now you can see that
imagination creates an enlargement and vivification
of reality that can be experienced anywhere, anytime,
anyplace. Imagination gives us a special way of
seeing that permits the extraordinary to exist in
exactly the same space that is totally occupied by
the ordinary. People who are centered don't just
experience or just imagine--they must experience
imaginatively!

FOOTNOTES - CHAPTER VI

[1] James Baldwin, "Notes of a Native Son, quoted by Dalton H. McBee, Writer's Journal: Explorations (New York: Harcourt Brace Jovanovich, Inc., 1972), 283.

[2] Henry David Thoreau, Walden and Other Writings (New York: The Modern Library, 1937), 86.

[3] Includes quote below and entire discussion of "Fabulous Realities" concept and exercises: Ken MacCrorie, Writing to be Read (New York: Hayden Book Co., Inc., 1978), 44-50.

[4] May Swenson, "A Boy on Looking at Big David," To Mix with Time (New York: Charles Scribner's Sons, 1963), 36.

[5] Sidney Cox, Indirections (New York: Viking, 1962), 6.

[6] May Swenson, "The Centaur," To Mix with Time, 86.

[7] Peter Elbow, Uptaught, quoted at Breadloaf Writer's Conference, Middlebury, Vermont, Summer, 1978.

[8] MacCrorie, 34.

[9] MacCrorie, 32-33.

[10] MacCrorie, 35-38. This entry covers the two poems and the discussions of the poems..

[11] Ira Progoff, At a Journal Workshop (New York: Dialogue House Library, 1975), 102.

[12] Progoff, 102-03.

[13] An adaptation to Progoff's "Time-Stretching" and "Steppingstones" exercises, 102-57.

[14] Suggested by a meditation exercise led by Ram Dass at the Yoga Institute, Houston, Texas, 1980.

[15] C. Hugh Holman, "Empathy," Handbook to Literature, 4th Edition (Indianapolis: Bobbs-Merrill Educational Publishing, 1980), 154.

[16] John Haynes, "The Cauliflower," 31 New American Poets, Ron Schreiber, ed. (New York: Hill and Wang, 1969), 73.

[17] Charles Simic, "Stone," The Young American Poets, Paul Carroll, ed. (Chicago: Follett Publishing Co., 1968), 390.

[18] Victor Contoski, "Money," 31 New American Poets, 26-27.

[19] An adaptation of Laura Huxley's exercise in You Are Not The Target (North Hollywood, CA: Wilshire Book Co., 1963), 52-55.

[20] Jane Shore, "Ararat," distributed at a poetry workshop, Houston, Texas, Spring, 1981.

[21] Jane Shore, "The Lifeguard," distributed at a poetry workshop, Houston, Texas, Spring, 1981.

[22] Holman, 12.

[23] "Allusion," Princeton Encyclopedia of Poetry and Poetics, Alex Preminger, ed. (Princeton, N.J.: Princeton University Press, 19 4), 18.

[24] May Sarton, "The Muse as Medusa," Selected Poems of May Sarton (New York: W. W. Norton and Co., Inc., 1978), 160.

[25] May Sarton, "At Delphi," Selected Poems, 162.

[26] John Gill, "The Other Garden," 31 New American Poets, 70.

[27] May Sarton, "Narcissus," Selected Poems, 168.

[28] May Sarton, "The Return of Aphrodite," Selected Poems, 169.

PUTTING IT ALL TOGETHER: FORMING THE WHOLE

Writing is a strange process: It begins as a
vague abstract (a thought or a feeling), confronted
by a blank page, then it becomes words sitting nakedly
on a page, then--if it is good, it becomes a rish,
whole experience. Here is such a poem by James
Dickey:

A SCREENED PORCH IN THE COUNTRY

All of them are sitting
Inside a lamp of coarse wire
And being in all directions
Shed upon darkness,
Their bodies softening to shadow, until
They come to rest out in the yard
In a kind of blurred golden country
In which they more deeply lie
Than if they were being created
Of heavenly light.

Where they are floating beyond
Themselves, in peace,
Where they have laid down
Their souls and not known it,
The smallest creatures,
As every night they do,
Come to the edge of them
And sing, if they can,
Or, if they can't, simply shine
Their eyes back, sitting on haunches.

Pulsating and thinking of music.
Occasionally, something weightless
Touches the screen
With its body, dies,
Or is unmurmuringly hurt,
But mainly nothing happens
Except that a family continues
To be laid down
In the midst of its nightly creatures,
Not on of which openly comes
Into the golden shadow
Where the people are lying,
Emitted by their own house
So humanly that they become
More than human, and enter the place

Of small, blindly singing things,
Seeming to rejoice
Perpetually, without effort,
Without knowing why
Or how they do it.[1]

--James Dickey

This poem, like the people on the screened porch,
makes its own golden glow. It catches something of
the mystery of life and of the interrelatedness of
life--mellow summer evenings, screened porches,
softening shadows and singing night creatures, and
the people "floating beyond themselves, in peace,
where they have laid down their souls and not known
it." Dickey sees that the sum of these experiences
adds up to our lives . . . and it is this realization
that this book is about . . . writing is not the
point--the products of the experiences are not the
point. The point is that by doing the exercises,
doing the writing, you may develop an active awareness
of the experiences of your outer and inner worlds that
results in a centeredness. By bridging the left and
right hemispheres of the brain, by balancing word
with image/symbol, concept with percept, fact with
dream, logic with memory, part with whole, we do indeed
float beyond ourselves, in peace, to find that place
where we laid down our souls without knowing it. . . .
Balancing, centering, is the process of learning to
know it, understanding the significance of our inner
and outer experience, of each moment, in all of its
wholeness. The value of experience doesn't depend on
what happens as much as it depends on what you do
with what happens, what you perceive to be the significance of what happens. What Dickey did through his
poem is share his very uncommon response to his
experience. First, he was in tune with his senses--he
perceived through his senses the facts of the moment.
Second, he was insightful--he used his imagination
and insight as the medium of "seeing" awarely that
experience. Third, he saw with double vision--he
perceived in that moment the relationship between the
usual and the unusual, the temporal and the universal,
and in so doing, he perceived the significance of that
moment. He was centered. And fourth, he put his
perceptions into words and shared with us the insights
and intensity of the original experience. In short,
his experience emerged as the statement about the
significance of a moment perceptively experienced.

So--the act of writing, of making experiences out of blank pages, is an uncommon act, a strange, mysterious thing to do. But, e.e. cummings says:

> . . . poems are for you and me
> and are not for most people . . .
> it's no use trying to pretend that
> most people and ourselves are alike.
> You and I are human beings; most
> people are snobs . . . If most people
> were to be born twice, they'd probably
> call it dying. With you I leave
> (in the form of poems) a remembrance
> of miracles: they are by somebody
> who can love and who shall be
> continually reborn . . .[2]

But writing is no more an uncommon act than centering. It is through centering that we write, and through writing that we are given one way to learn to be centered. Writing gives us a focus for the awareness of the miracles in our experience and in our world; and centering awakens us to the fact that nobody can be you but you--nobody can sense, imagine, remember, perceive as you can--nobody can see what you "see." Centering allows us--you and me--to recognize our special way of seeing and our special gift of saying what we see--and because of these gifts, we shall be continually reborn--with each moment we experience through a centered mind, body, and soul.

FOOTNOTES - EPILOGUE

[1] James Dickey, "A Screened Porch in the Country," Poems 1957-1967 (New York: Collier Books, 1967), 96.

[2] e. e. cummings, "Preface," 95 Poems (New York: Harcourt, Brace and World, Inc. 1958), i.

ABOUT THE AUTHOR

Margaret Hatcher, Ed.D., is the Superintendent of Schools in Telluride, Colorado. She has been a teacher for twenty years on both the secondary and university levels, and she has held various administrative posts. Her interest in brain research and its implications to education began when she was teacher/coordinator at the High School for Performing and Visual Arts in Houston, Texas, where she witnessed dramatic increases in academic achievement when tasks were coupled with creative right-brain techniques. Since then, she has been involved in the research and study of improved methods of educating the whole person: mind, body and spirit. She believes that brain research can provide educators with valuable keys to restoring the quality of education and and the joy of learning in schools.